OBSERVATIONS
FROM A RECOVERING
ALCOHOLIC

OBSERVATIONS
FROM A RECOVERING
ALCOHOLIC

DR. J. ANTHONY QUINN

Why Human Connection Is
More Important Than Ever

WELLSPRING

North Palm Beach, Florida

wellspring

Copyright © 2022
Published by WELLSPRING

Design by Ashley Dias

ISBN: 978-1-63582-249-6 (hardcover)

10   9   8   7   6   5   4   3   2   1

Printed in the United States of America

CONTENTS

INTRODUCTION

This is a message of hope and passion regarding my experience living a sober lifestyle. I am not in any way a representative of or spokesperson for an organization or group. I simply wish to share my personal experience of how a 12-step program positively impacted my life and the lives of so many around me. My motive is to share the story of my journey with sobriety and what I have personally experienced going through a 12-step program. This is not meant to be an attack on other methods of achieving sobriety; it's a compassionate plea to acknowledge a system that has worked for so many.

Lately there are those who say this program is obsolete, that with the advancement of neuroscience, the 12 steps no longer apply. The pharmaceutical industry has become deeply involved in addiction medicine and is promoting drug therapy for the treatment of addiction. Medication-assisted treatment (MAT) is the use of medications in combination with behavioral therapies for the treatment of substance abuse disorders. Drugs are utilized to reduce cravings or withdrawal symptoms. As I will discuss later, these drugs can be very helpful, but it is my concern that they risk being misused as a solution to long-term sobriety.

Recently I was given a copy of the New York State Office of Addiction Services and Supports' (OASAS) "Standards for OASAS Certified Programs." New York State now promotes medication-assisted treatment for many of the professionals it monitors. I was told that this document is often used by other states in setting up their own programs. In describing recovery, it reads, "Treatment goals should focus on impairment and distress caused by substance use. A person may be in remission from their substance use disorder and still use substances. Individuals should meet milestones in treatment established in the treatment/recovery plan. The treatment plan goal is the person achieving recovery; it is for the patient to determine what recovery is and how it is defined."[1] I find this statement puzzling—it seems illogical for a person who has an addictive mind to decide how recovery should be defined. I needed help to become sober. If it had been up to me to define recovery, I would have thought that maybe I would not drink from Monday to Thursday, but it would be all right to drink on weekends. In my case that would not have been possible. Although medication-assisted treatment is an important step in saving the addict from killing him or herself during the dangerous and acute stage of early recovery, it can't be a bridge to nowhere; it must lead the addict to a space where a foundation of sobriety can be created.

It is my hope that by sharing some of my experiences as well as the experiences of others, I can illustrate just how complex this illness is and how much attention must be given to it if one is to become healthy. If it were about drinking or drugs alone, then all we would have to do is stop the use. It is, however, a thinking disorder combined with a physical addiction. For the addict, the use of alcohol or drugs relieves, even if only for a short time, the uncomfortable feelings of being an alcoholic. Using another drug to relieve the urge to use, although helpful, is not what being sober is about. I believe that this illness requires one's full attention. It is a daily commitment to steps that, if followed, can lead to a life of purpose and happiness.

If the intent of MAT is harm reduction in hopes that the addict will eventually get sober, then we need to accept that for what it is. It is not sobriety; it is a step in that direction. The same pharmaceutical industry that produced much of the medication that caused addiction in millions of people is now supplying the answer with more drugs. I am skeptical. We will learn that in the latest studies, Alcoholics Anonymous has been shown to be the most effective path to long-term sobriety.

My deepest concern is that we are going to go down the same path we did with antidepressants. Treating depression with medication was supposed to be a short-term drug intervention strategy. Unfortunately, for many it has become long-term drug use resulting in addiction and, for those who try to stop, withdrawal.

Our sobriety is only as strong as the systems we use daily. I am not arguing that a 12-step program is infallible or fits all situations. For example, recently a friend of mine relapsed on cocaine and heroin after thirty-four years of on-again, off-again sobriety. Over those years he has relapsed a dozen times. He is now back in treatment. If I were negative about this, I could say that AA is a failure. Yet if this were cancer and he had a recurrence of his disease, we would address it and not call it a failure. If I look at it in a positive way, then I have to recognize that of those thirty-four years he has had almost thirty years of being sober.

USA Today reported in March 2020 on a new study

showing the effectiveness of Alcoholics Anonymous. According to the article, Alcoholics Anonymous "has long been criticized for not having the medical research to back up its efficacy. Until now."[2]

The study, published by the medical journal *Cochrane Database of Systematic Review*, found the peer-led program not only helps people get sober, but it also has higher rates of continuous sobriety compared with professional mental health therapy, such as cognitive behavioral therapy.[3]

This is important because it dispels misinformation about the program, said lead author Dr. John Kelly, a professor of psychiatry and addiction medicine at Harvard Medical School.

The article goes on to state, "In the popular press, there's been reports of AA not working or being harmful for people," he said. "So, we wanted to clarify the scientific picture to the highest scientific standard.

The study had the opposite findings of a similar study published by Cochrane in 2006 that found "no experimental studies unequivocally demonstrated the effectiveness of AA or TSF (twelve-step facilitation) approaches for reducing alcohol dependence of problems.

The 2006 review included eight trials with about 3,400

people, while the new review included 27 studies of more than 10,500 people.

The studies reviewed and rated AA`s effectiveness by measuring factors including the length of time participants abstained from alcohol, the amount they reduced their drinking, if they continued drinking, the consequences of their drinking and their health care costs.

AA was never found less effective and was often significantly better than other interventions or quitting cold turkey. One study found the program 60% more effective than alternatives."

Psychologist Keith Humphreys, co-author of the study and a Stanford University psychiatry professor, said mental health professionals—early in his career—are frequently skeptical of AA`s effectiveness. Psychologists and psychiatrists are often trained to provide cognitive behavior therapy and motivational enhancement therapy to treat patients with alcohol abuse disorder.

He recalled thinking, "how dare these people do things that I have all these degrees to do".

The article goes on to state. "AA didn`t come from the scientific community, it came from people who were suffering addiction. They`re just people with a lived experience[4] and that`s powerful when you multiply that by a couple of million people."

The study found higher rates in long term sobriety when medical professionals connected their patients to AA after completing a 12- step program.[5]

WHAT IS ALCOHOLISM?

"One of the most important facts to remember about alcoholism is its progression. Alcoholism begins in an early stage that looks nothing at all like a life-threatening disease, proceeds into a middle stage where problems begin to appear and intensify, and gradually advances into the late, degenerative stages of obvious physiological dependence, physical and psychological deterioration, and loss of control."
— *William F. Asbury*, Beyond the Influence

Let me share two stories to help explain alcoholism. The first is about a brilliant friend of mine who about thirty years ago was diagnosed with virally induced acute pancreatitis. His pancreas was enlarged and severely inflamed. It was not due to alcohol but caused by a viral infection.

After a stay in the hospital, he had an office visit with his physician, who told him that there was probably some damage to his pancreas and that it would be a good idea if he avoided alcohol. He has not had a drink since that day, more than thirty years ago.

The second story is about a highly trained health care professional who was hospitalized with pancreatitis ten years ago due to excessive alcohol consumption. He recovered and was advised by his physician to avoid alcohol. Ignoring his doctor's advice, he resumed drinking and shortly thereafter was back in the hospital with a more severe case of pancreatitis. This time he checked himself out of the hospital against medical advice and took a taxi to a bar. After becoming sick yet again, he was put into rehab. The treatment failed and he drank again. That is alcoholism. Fortunately for him, after two rehabs and a few relapses, he has been sober for the past five years.

Alcoholism is a disease of the mind. The first gentleman was not an alcoholic and had complete awareness of himself and his body. When he was told that drinking was dangerous to his health, his mind noted it and made a rational decision. The health care professional, when told that his pancreatitis was caused by alcohol, simply blocked that information out and made an irrational decision that he could still consume alcohol. It defies logic.

Logic is not a tool the alcoholic is familiar with. To protect the illness, he has to rationalize, using his own flawed thinking to get to the desired end. Whereas a normally thinking person would view an alcoholic's conclusion as bizarre, the alcoholic can somehow weave a web of self-deceit to get to the desired conclusion. We can get home at four a.m. with what seems like a perfectly reasonable answer for doing so. It is almost as if we have to work backward. It is baffling, and to break down that powerful defense takes an enormous effort on the part of those charged with the task. When I look back at my own flawed, illogical thinking, I am amazed that I was unable to recognize it until I was removed from the insanity of my behavior and given enough time to listen and contemplate. That ability to rationalize stays with the alcoholic, and he must always guard against it and its ability to convince him that taking a drink again will not be harmful.

ANXIETY IS AN INTEGRAL PART OF ALCOHOLISM

"Worrying is carrying tomorrow's load with today's strength—carrying two days at once. It is moving into tomorrow ahead of time. Worrying doesn't empty tomorrow of its sorrow, it empties today of its strength."
— *Corrie ten Boom*

I was born into a large Irish Catholic family. As the first-born, I felt like there were high expectations of me; I was certain that I was expected to succeed, to be a good example, and not to let my parents or family down in any aspect of my life.

To this day I remember walking to the Nativity grade school with my aunt, who was kind enough to take me to my first day of first grade, because my mother had four small children at home. I was filled with dread all the way, and I did not want to go into the school. I never gave it much thought until years after I became sober. I was anxious, and I realized that that anxiety played a major role in my life for the first forty-plus years of my life. My father pushed me because he was not going to let me fail, and as his firstborn, I was going to lead my brothers and sisters by my success. It was a recipe for disaster, at least internally.

Early on I was a good student—not great, merely good. That was not acceptable to my father, because he wanted me to excel. My anxiety made it difficult for me to concentrate, so at the blackboard on the wall in our kitchen, as I was trying to learn my times tables, I could not get the right answer to 8 times 7. I knew the answer, but I had too much anxiety to see it. This only frustrated my father, who had no idea of my underlying fear, and this led to even more anxiety. He would tell me to "just think." I could not; I was too overwhelmed. I learned to manage the anxiety or at least not show it, but it never really left until I found alcohol.

That first drink or drug is magical for those starting on the path of addiction. I have heard the same story a thousand times. All the fears and anxieties melt away with that first drinking experience, and we all chase that initial feeling for the rest of our drinking or drugging careers. What is most interesting is that we never have that feeling again, but we just cannot stop chasing it.

It occurred to me why so many addicts have such a clear memory of the first drink or drug. I have never met an alcoholic who did not suffer from some form of anxiety. That first exposure and the lifting of that feeling is over-whelming, and we pursue the repeat of that experience until we die or realize it is the lie of addiction.

MY EXPERIENCE

"I realized that I only had two choices: I was either going to die or I was going to live, and which one did I want to do? And then I said those words, 'I'll get help,' or, 'I need help. I'll get help.' And my life turned around.'"
— *Sir Elton John*

When I went into a treatment center in 1986, there were two basic programs for addiction: twenty-eight days for alcohol and forty-two days for drug addiction. My drug of choice was alcohol, but toward the end of my run, I became addicted to cocaine; I thought it gave me clarity while I was drinking. Cocaine in the early 1980s was considered a recreational drug by many in my circle. That was all I needed to hear; "recreational" sounds so harmless. So, from 1983 until 1986 I had my own "department of recreation." That cocaine experience sped my descent and eventually landed me in rehab. Today I am grateful for that experience, because if I'd continued on alcohol only, I may have wasted more years in the prison of addiction.

By the time I entered treatment, my thinking was completely distorted. It was a desire to stay sober and to use all wrapped up together, each desire battling for a position. When I left the facility, my thinking had changed but was still far from where it should have been. I knew I had a problem and couldn't use successfully, but maybe, just maybe, there was a way. The thoughts of "successful" drinking occupied my mind all day. If I had been able to select my own version of treatment or recovery, I think I would have suggested a one-day, three-hour course on how to drink successfully without consequences. It certainly would not have been longer than twenty-four hours.

When I first landed in treatment, I thought I would stay for a week and then the physicians and counselors would realize I was not that bad. I was convinced that now that I was aware of the situation, I would be perfectly capable of addressing the issues on my own. Then I thought that for sure I would be released at the end of twenty-eight days. I was not. The "authorities" told me that I would be staying for the full forty-two days. I was furious! How dare they judge me? The alcoholic part of my brain told me that I did not need so much treatment. The real me, the humble and honest me, knew that they were right, and deep down

I saw the truth of my predicament, so I agreed to stay. Where was I going to go? Back to what life? My life was falling apart outside those walls, my family was in disarray. I was in a practice of Orthodontics with two other orthodontists who were supportive but understandingly wary. I had to show my partners that I was not a risk. Deciding to remain in treatment was the best decision I could have made to assure them that I was serious about facing up to my addiction.

It was during those last two weeks that I was finally able to see reality instead of a distorted world where I thought everyone was just trying to get me to stop drinking. I no longer believed that I just had a drinking problem; I saw that I had a *living* problem. I believe that I have remained sober because of the wisdom of that treatment team. Those last two weeks are when I finally realized just how sick I was.

It is a very different treatment landscape today. Now treatment team coordinators are lucky if they can secure seven days of inpatient treatment. These decisions are made at the intersection of money and insurance company policy. Insurance companies basically do not want to pay for inpatient treatment. (As so many of us have experienced, this is also true for general hospital inpatient care.) The insurance companies may justify these policies because of the small percentage of overtreatment within the industry, but this does not tell the full story. Outpatient therapy is, in many cases, simply not enough time for a successful course of treatment. Statistics for recovery are not always accurate because of the difficulty in following former patients over the long term. On top of that, if someone has returned to drinking or using, they will not always be completely honest.

Many have stated that the US health care system is based not on preventive medicine but on "sickness care." We wait until the end of a cycle to spend money. It is fascinating to me that we are willing to spend huge sums of money to extend one's life a couple of months with very expensive treatments at the end of life, yet we will not invest in the treatment of people in their twenties, thirties, and forties who could have many years of productive life left. To paraphrase the comedian Trevor Noah, Americans live in a society that ignores the "check engine light." We wait until the car is on fire to do something.

I have been taught that alcoholism is a thinking disease, not just a drinking or drug disease. The self-administration of alcohol and drugs results in tremendous physical, mental, and spiritual damage. By spiritual, I don't mean religious, but that core sense of worth and value that connects us to one another. The action of putting down the substance is only the beginning. As it is written in the book Alcoholics Anonymous, now that we've put the drink down, the real work begins. Adding medication may help temporarily, but there is little chance of achieving any true self-awareness in the long term. As I will point out, we tried this with antidepressants, and although they helped, they were never supposed to be long term. As with all chronic illnesses, the first treatment may not work or may work for only a short time, but we continue to treat the patient. Why do we so often give up on mental health and addiction?

Over the years, I have met and worked with many people involved in treatment centers. Most of those I have met are overworked, underpaid, and completely dedicated to their patients. I have talked to many addiction doctors who have spent countless hours trying to convince insurance companies to give patients enough time. It is a difficult, demanding, frustrating task to try to get adequate treatment time for patients who desperately need it to heal, yet these doctors persist.

Dr. David Withers, a former medical director of Geisinger Marworth Treatment Center, in Pennsylvania, often would say to a new patient upon arrival, "What happened to you is truly tragic. You can be defined by that tragedy, or you can be defined by how you respond to it." The problem is that very often alcoholics tend to want to become the victim—if they do, they will remain in the tragedy.

MEDICATION-ASSISTED TREATMENT

*"I have been practicing Addiction Medicine for
20 years and on some days I just feel like a drug dealer
wearing a white coat."*
— Dr. David K., Recovering Physician

As I indicated earlier, I am in favor of medication-assisted treatment (MAT), but I am concerned that we are now on a slippery slope of turning a whole population into mildly addicted people. The preferred goal of treatment for alcoholics and addicts is abstinence, which in my opinion leads to a clear mind and awareness. Addiction is not simply about alcohol and drugs—it is about our thought patterns, and until the patient's thinking is addressed, we simply cannot start on a path of recovery.

With the current opioid crisis, there is no question that medication is necessary to help slow down the epidemic of overdosing and death that has ravaged the United States. This medication-assisted treatment is absolutely necessary in the early treatment of some addicts. The term *harm reduction* is being used to describe this approach. In the early stages of treatment of an opioid addict, it may be imperative to use buprenorphine or methadone to wean the patient from opioids and help prevent an overdose death. Naloxone, an opioid antagonist that reverses the effects of narcotics, is also used. Buprenorphine is a partial agonist; methadone is a full agonist, meaning it mimics the effect of opioids, such as heroin, in the brain. However, this approach is not the answer to long-term sobriety, because first, it doesn't address the root of addiction; second, patients may become dependent on the MAT drugs; and finally, there are many unpleasant side effects. Common side effects of buprenorphine, for example, include dizziness, drowsiness, blurred vision, feeling drunk, trouble concentrating, tongue pain, redness or numbness inside the mouth, nausea, vomiting, constipation, headache, back pain, fast or pounding heartbeat, increased sweating, and sleep problems such as insomnia. This drug is a narcotic, and although it should be dispensed by a trained physician, it is also being sold illegally on the street.

Currently in Pennsylvania, addicts must agree to behavioral treatment if they are to receive drug therapy. In my discussions with four physician addiction specialists, all of whom are also in long-term recovery, they have reported that most of the patients simply comply in order to get their drugs. There are those who are serious about recovery, but they are in the minority. If the purpose is harm reduction, then these programs are very effective, but if we are looking for long-term recovery, this may not be the answer. It is possible that we will create a whole population on long-term medication-assisted treatment, with patients trading one drug for another.

There has been some debate as to whether professionals such as surgeons, airline pilots, and anesthesiologists should be allowed to work while on MAT. It may be appropriate to use this treatment early in their recovery, before they return to work. I have been told by a former board member of the Pennsylvania Physicians' Health Program that lawyers are threatening the board with lawsuits if they prevent a professional from returning to work while on medication-assisted treatment. There are those who think that people involved in critical care should be completely free of any mind-altering medication. I would be concerned if my anesthesiologist, surgeon, or pilot were taking any opioid medications. Patients on these drugs can be impaired, even if only slightly. In my opinion it is only after they have been weaned off and are working a program and being monitored that they can be allowed to be responsible for the lives of others.

Americans are by far the world's largest consumers of pharmaceutical drugs, and yet we are neither the happiest nor the healthiest population. You need only to watch television or use the internet to see how we are bombarded with ads (always running longer than a normal advertisement) promoting health and happiness through drugs. We have been conditioned by these pharmaceutical companies to believe that if there is a problem, then there must be a drug for it. If people took the time to read the inserts listing the number of possible side effects, they might be hesitant to use some of these medications.

The pharmaceutical industry has created some amazing drugs that have saved many and altered the lives of people with serious and sometimes fatal illnesses, and it should be rewarded for the research and development of these lifesaving drugs. There is, however, a dark side to the industry (remember the price gouging for the EpiPen?). *The Washington Post* reported that more than 100 billion pills saturated the United States over a nine-year period, igniting the opioid crisis. The DEA revealed that this was 24 billion pills more than was previously known to the public. This is the same industry that originally reported that opioids are not addictive.

I am not minimizing the importance of medication for the treatment of serious illnesses. What I intend to show is that alcoholism is a complex illness that needs much more than medication for its sufferers to have a chance to survive, and that the 12 steps are as relevant today as they were in 1939, when the book *Alcoholics Anonymous* was first published. We were warned more than eighty years ago not to look for an easier, softer way, and it appears to me that that is exactly what we are doing.

THE 12 STEPS

"The mentality and behavior of drug addicts and alcoholics is wholly irrational until you understand that they are completely powerless over their addiction, and unless they have structured help, they have no hope."
— Russell Brand

For those not familiar with them, here are the 12 steps of *Alcoholics Anonymous*:

- **Step 1**: Admit we are powerless over alcohol—that our lives have become unmanageable.
- **Step 2**: Come to believe that a power greater than us can restore us to sanity.
- **Step 3**: Make a decision to turn our will and our lives over to the care of God, *as we understand him*.
- **Step 4**: Make a searching and fearless moral inventory of ourselves.
- **Step 5**: Admit to God, to ourselves, and to another human being the exact nature of our wrongs.
- **Step 6**: We are entirely ready to have God remove all these defects of character.

- **Step** 7: Humbly ask God to remove our shortcomings.
- **Step 8**: Make a list of all persons we have harmed and become willing to make amends to them all.
- **Step 9**: Make direct amends to such people wherever possible, except when to do so would injure them or others.
- **Step 10**: Continue to take personal inventory and when we are wrong promptly admit it.
- **Step 11**: Seek through prayer and meditation to improve our conscious contact with God *as we understand him*, praying only for knowledge of his will for us and the power to carry that out.
- **Step 12**: Having had a spiritual awakening as a result of the steps, we try to carry this message to alcoholics, and to practice these principles in all our affairs.

The authors of the steps spent a great deal of time formulating these steps and they were done in a specific order. Each step was to be completed before moving on to the next one and they were to be done with another recovering person who could facilitate and make sure that they were completed successfully.

ALCOHOL, THE DRUG

*"Because alcohol is encouraged by our culture,
we get the idea that it isn't dangerous. However, alcohol
is the most potent and most toxic of the
legal psychoactive drugs."*
— Beverly A. Potter & Sebastian Orfali

Many people think of alcohol as a stimulant, but actually it is classed as a depressant. As such, it slows down vital functions, which eventually results in slurred speech, uncoordinated movement, disturbed perception, and an inability to react appropriately.

A small amount of alcohol can initially feel like a stimulant. It reduces anxiety, makes one feel more comfortable, and makes it easier to interact with others. I am sure most people notice that a social setting such as a cocktail party usually starts off slow and a bit quiet, but after a few drinks the noise level increases as people become more comfortable. The vast majority of people will have one or two drinks for that social lubricant; however, there are about 10 percent of the population who have an "allergy" to alcohol. They, like me, cannot have just one or two, and they use alcohol until it becomes a depressant and causes numerous physical, social, and mental problems.

Pure alcohol is poison to the human body and can lead to death. It can be used as a solvent, paint remover, or a topical antiseptic. The National Institutes of Health (NIH) launched a study in 2014 to determine whether moderate drinking protects heart health. It was shut down in 2018 when it was revealed that NIH officials had lobbied beer and liquor companies for funding and suggested that the results of the trial would support moderate drinking.[6]

I have a brother, a surgeon, who at one time was the physician responsible for dealing with the examiners when the hospital he worked in was being evaluated for accreditation by the Joint Commission. The evaluator was a rather stern nurse, and they were walking through the operating room when the nurse turned to my brother and said, "Exactly what are you using to disinfect the operating room?"

He could not remember the name of the product, so he replied, "Alcohol."

She stopped and turned to him and said, "Doctor, alcohol will not kill anything."

He responded, "I beg your pardon, but alcohol killed half of my family."

Alcohol has been with humans for a long time. It has been embraced and banned. Banning it has never worked, so the government decided that if alcohol was going to be used by society, then it would have to be managed with laws and licenses. The truth is that alcohol is a money-maker for the government.

The state allows for a drug to be self-administered. It is taxed and managed. That same model is being used with marijuana today. The government could not control the illegal use of the drug, so it decided to get in the business of licensing its production, sale, and distribution for self-administration. Because of the ability to manipulate plant genetics it is now possible to grow even more potent marijuana plants than ever before. We use terms like *medical marijuana* to distinguish it from recreational use. The problem is that marijuana makes almost everybody feel better. There is no question that it is helpful in reducing pain and anxiety but trying to determine who actually qualifies for medicinal use is a bit tricky.

As I said, the potency of marijuana used today is quite different than what was on the street years ago. Today`s marijuana is considerably more potent. Because of that, there have been some serious consequences with its use, particularly for young people. Although there is debate among the experts, cannabis-induced psychosis and schizophrenia in teenagers and young adults are on the rise because of the drug's increased use. Like alcohol, marijuana is not a harmless drug. People who are not susceptible to addiction may be able to use it moderately, but for those of us who are susceptible it is just another unfortunate path to misery.

While visiting some family members in Colorado a few years ago, we were taking off in a small private plane in a rural airport, and we noticed a spectacular three-story building off to the side of the runway. On the plane, I asked the pilot what the building was, and he told me it was for their local volunteer fire department. He went on to say that the state had made so much money from the sale of marijuana that they told the fire department to build whatever they wanted, hence the most beautiful fire station I have ever seen.

If the government is going to benefit from the distribution and sale of drugs, then I believe it should also be responsible for the treatment of those who become addicted.

ALCOHOLISM

"An alcoholic is someone who can violate his standards
faster than he can lower them."
— Robin Williams

Most professionals agree that alcoholism is a chronic, progressive, fatal illness that is treatable in almost all cases. Common thought is that if only the alcoholic would stop drinking, then things would improve. Unfortunately, simply putting the drink down does not relieve the alcoholic of his or her alcoholic thinking. We have been taught in the 12 steps that drinking is only a symptom of our alcoholism. This is a chronic disease, and as such it needs daily attention. We are given only twenty-four hours. We wake up as an alcoholic every day, and because of that, we must do what is suggested to maintain our health.

Alcoholism and diabetes are chronic illnesses that have much in common. The diabetic wakes up every day a diabetic and cannot rely on yesterday's health as a guarantee of todays. He must take action steps: check his blood sugar, eat properly, and take insulin if necessary. These action steps will keep him from the disastrous, life-threatening effects of his illness. Without these daily steps the disease will progress and eventually be fatal. As an alcoholic I must also take action steps: go to a meeting, call my sponsor, pray and meditate, read something about my condition, and reach out and help someone who is struggling. All these positive actions will help me to maintain the gift of my sobriety.

A friend of mine spent many years working as a drug rep for diabetes medication. She told me that many physicians have difficulty treating diabetics, because they do not follow directions and as a result experience organ damage. She explained that many diabetics will take their insulin daily, and when they start to feel better, they stop. Alcoholics are very similar. The addict stops drinking or using drugs and starts to follow directions. Life gets better. Soon the addict thinks that she is OK and no longer needs help. She stops going to meetings and talking to other recovering people, and she returns to the most dangerous place for an alcoholic: inside her own head. We were warned by Bill Wilson, who wrote the original draft of *Alcoholics Anonymous*, that if we stop doing the steps of recovery, the ancient enemy of the alcoholic will eventually return: rationalization. By herself the alcoholic is eventually going to talk herself into picking up a drink.

The strategies for treating alcoholics have been controversial since the very beginning. At first alcoholics were placed in sanitoriums, sometimes even put in straitjackets, as was the experience of one of my aunts, in hopes that she would somehow "dry out" and then recover. It didn't work. After two weeks of drying out, she was released. She returned home and started to drink, and it was not long after that she died from the damage to her organs caused by alcohol. She was fifty-four years old.

The first groups who tried to help alcoholics were religious based, which in itself caused controversy. Bill Wilson and the other founders knew that this would be a problem and agonized over the wording of the 12 steps. They finally agreed to say that the alcoholic would just have to accept a power greater than himself, no matter who that power was. It was believed that alcoholism is a physical, emotional, and spiritual illness. It is important to remember that *spiritual* does not mean religious. We are now in the age of neuroscience, with a belief that addiction is biochemical and that manipulating the biochemistry of the brain can relieve this illness. Some have postulated that seeking a source of power outside yourself is a sign of weakness. When I discussed this with a friend of mine, a counselor in a rehabilitation center, he offered me his two-thousand-dollar collection of tapes, including all of Tony Robbins' tapes and CDs. He had spent two years listening to motivational speakers to try to control his drinking. It wasn't until he surrendered and went to treatment that he finally became sober.

Drugs are now being used to relieve the alcoholic and drug addict of the compulsion to drink or use. Like the diabetic has insulin to help break down sugar, the alcoholic has drugs to treat the cravings, but we are still left with the flawed thinking pattern of the person. In both instances the patient does not always comply. If we believe that alcoholism is a thinking illness, then recovery is more than just abstinence. AA is not perfect, but it has provided a map for millions of people to follow in order to achieve and maintain recovery. The problem is that many don't stay on the path.

There have been many attempts to teach people how to drink successfully with this illness, including Rational Recovery, cognitive behavior therapy, moderation drinking, and biofeedback. Many of these attempts were used to try to teach alcoholics to drink normally. One of the latest is Sober Curious, in which you are sort of sober. If you are simply an abuser of drugs and alcohol, then these programs can be helpful. If you are truly an alcoholic, however, the success rate is questionable. Although access to accurate statistics for all these programs is hard to obtain, I do know that many of them have fallen by the wayside. I have to remember that all alcoholics and addicts harbor the thought, no matter how much pain they have suffered or caused, that somehow they can drink or use successfully. That thought stays hidden in the brain of the addict and reemerges when we are not spiritually fit. Maybe someday there will be a pill or shot to relieve us of this thinking disorder—I would consider it—but until then, we have to use the best way available for us to continue on this path of recovery. I do not want to replace one drug with another, so I'm hesitant to use medication-assisted therapy long term to relieve me of this illness.

If one is truly alcoholic there is simply no easy way out. In order to survive, he or she must find a completely new way of living.

On average, let's say an alcoholic drinks for about twenty hours a week. He or she never complains about the amount of time spent doing so, yet the idea of doing three to five hours of Alcoholics Anonymous meetings a week seems overwhelming. Alcoholic thinking is that powerful.

A BIT OF HISTORY

"The journey of a thousand miles begins with one step."
— *Lao-tzu*

I did not decide to write this book in defense of rehabilitation centers or 12-step programs. Nor am I writing
it in criticism of any other form of treatment. Addiction
is an extremely difficult illness to treat no matter what
the protocol is. With the opioid crisis it has become even
more challenging. There are many ways to get sober, including inpatient treatment, Alcoholics Anonymous, psychological therapy, drug therapy, and recently introduced
apps. Whatever works is sufficient. However, I do believe
that long-term sobriety has to be about abstinence and,
just as important, contact with other recovering people.
In my opinion, the human connection is the answer to
long-term contentment. In an August 2012 *Psychology
Today* article titled "Connect to Thrive," Dr. Emma Seppälä states:

People who feel more connected to others have lower

rates of anxiety and depression. Moreover, studies show they also have higher self-esteem, are more empathic to others, more trusting and cooperative and, as a consequence, others are more open to trusting and cooperating with them. Social connectedness therefore generates a positive feedback loop of social, emotional and physical well-being. Unfortunately, the opposite is also true for those who lack social connectedness. Low social connection has been generally associated with declines in physical and psychological health as well as a higher propensity to antisocial behavior that leads to further isolation.[7]

To criticize 12-step program therapy and not see the value it has had for so many is unfair. Over the years that I have been sober, I have met many people who have sought that form of treatment and have been successful—some long term, some with intermittent relapses, but they continue to stay on the path to recovery. As the medical definition of alcoholism describes, this is a disease characterized by relapse.

In a June 2019 *New York Times* article, "The New Sobriety," Alex Williams writes about a new movement for those who are able to drink a little without serious consequences.[8] If you are an abuser of alcohol, then this is definitely possible. If you are an alcoholic as we understand it, then it is not. Alcoholics have been trying to find an easier, softer way since the beginning and it simply does not work, so confusing abuse with alcoholism is dangerous. Bill Wilson said if you are not certain, then try some controlled drinking—you will eventually find out which category you fall into.

I had plenty of classmates in college and professional school and fellow officers in the US Air Force who drank heavily and were into drugs. Many had what appeared to be serious addictions. To my surprise, most of them went through those phases and eventually either quit or became moderate alcohol and drug users. They were not alcoholics or addicts; they were abusers. Abuse is a period of time of heavy or addiction-like use, but it is not necessarily addiction. There are millions of people who have successfully taken opioids for valid reasons and have not become addicts. On the other side, there are those of us who are genetically predisposed to addiction and are simply more likely to become addicted. For us, alcohol or drugs cause an intense stimulation of the brain's reward system. This in turn unlocks a host of euphoric feelings and sometimes bizarre outcomes. This message to the brain is, "This is what you have been looking for," and from that day forward we chase that first experience.

Eighty years ago, when Bill Wilson and his friends wrote the text on alcoholism, they knew that the inability to successfully control our drinking was the issue at hand. If you are an alcoholic, then you have a progressive illness that does not go away or get better. It only gets worse with time. If you are an abuser, then you may be able to drink, but you have to find that out on your own. I had a very close friend whom I drank with through most of my drinking career. He drank and smoked more than I ever did and never stopped, until he died from the effects of alcohol and tobacco.

I never thought of him as an alcoholic. He did not have some of the personality traits of an alcoholic, like resentment and anger. He was a kind and gentle spirit, and he was not restless, irritable, or discontented. He was an abuser, not an alcoholic. But even abusers can suffer the effects of abusive drinking and an unhealthy lifestyle.

The recent introduction of drugs to curb cravings is extremely helpful for those who cannot seem to stay sober. I would hope that the goal for all medication-assisted treatment is to use it as a path to abstinence from any drugs. There are those who, unfortunately, cannot be honest with themselves, and their only option may be medication. They are not sober; they are on maintenance drug therapy, which in some cases may be the best we can hope for.

DRUGS FOR ANXIETY AND DEPRESSION

"Having anxiety and depression is like being scared and tired at the same time. It's the fear of failure, but no urge to be productive. It's wanting friends but hating socializing. It's wanting to be alone, but not wanting to be lonely. It's feeling everything at once [and] then feeling paralyzing numb."
— *Anonymous, Healthyplace.com*

Anxiety and depression are two very powerful mental conditions that can affect alcoholics and nonalcoholics alike. When a person is treated for alcoholism, it must be determined whether getting sober is enough to alleviate the symptoms of depression and anxiety or if the patient needs drug therapy as well.

When antidepressant drugs were first launched, they were touted as an answer to depression. Since they were introduced, millions of people have benefited from them. In 2018, the *New York Times* reported in an article titled "Many People Taking Antidepressants Discover They Cannot Quit" that long-term use of antidepressants is surging in the United States.[9] Some 15.5 million

Americans have been taking these medications for at least five years. The rate has exploded since 2000. According to the article, the drugs initially were approved for short-term use, typically about two months. What was designed for short-term use has become long-term drug therapy, and with that have come problems of addiction and then withdrawal when people try to stop taking the antidepressants. Yet again we have another drug that has been abused. What we thought was the answer to a problem, while helpful in many cases, created a whole new list of problems that we are just starting to recognize and address. Changing one's brain chemistry is not a simple long-term cure for addiction.

This was not the first-time addictive drugs were used to try to treat the alcoholic or addict. In the book *An Anatomy of Addiction: Sigmund Freud, William Halsted, and the Miracle Drug Cocaine*, Dr. Howard Markel recounts that Freud was introduced to cocaine in the early 1800s. He was convinced that the drug could be used to treat morphine addicts of that time. Not only that, but Freud also himself became addicted.[10] Well-intentioned physicians unwittingly turned many morphine addicts into cocaine addicts.

Dr. William Stewart Halsted, the famous American surgeon, was searching for an anesthetic that he could utilize in his surgical practice. He became addicted to cocaine and at one point sank into a drug-induced oblivion that lasted for seven months. Both doctors originally thought this drug could be used without long-term dependence.

Many physicians and pharmaceutical companies are now promoting drugs, although these are not as powerful. A number of these drugs are themselves addictive and are not the answer to addiction. Pharmaceutical companies realize that abstinence does not produce profit. This is not to say that we have not benefited from the advancements made with drug therapy, but again, more drugs are not the answer. Abstinence is not a profit center, but for the alcoholic it is the long-term goal. As with depression, pharmaceutical companies see an opportunity to generate enormous revenue from the treatment of addiction, and the longer the patient is on the drugs, the more revenue is generated.

Let's take a brief look at tobacco companies. When they were pushing smoking early on, one of their ad campaigns was "My doctor smokes Camels," and for years they distorted science, saying tobacco did not cause cancer. When vaping was developed, the vaping companies told us it was to help people quit smoking—while delivering nicotine directly to the lungs. Meanwhile, flavors were added so they could hook children. Recently the Trump administration with great fanfare announced that it would ban vaping flavors and protect our children from becoming addicted. Ultimately, only the three least utilized flavors were banned, while menthol—the most popular flavor—continues to be sold. Menthol creates a cooling effect, reduces the harshness of smoke, and suppresses coughing, which makes the flavor more appealing to young people. We were told that the government allowed the vaping companies to continue to sell the poison to protect the vaping industry. No regulations were placed on disposable vaping instruments, so vaping by our most vulnerable young people continues unabated, as does the dishonesty of the industry.

When the battle over smoking was going on, this same argument was used to protect the tobacco industry. There was great concern about tobacco farmers and the economic harm to the industry. Then it was discovered that the tobacco companies had a goal of addicting three thousand people a day to replace the three thousand who were dying every day from the effects of smoking. As always, it is about money. Tobacco companies have bought into vaping, and the vaping companies are utilizing the same misleading tactics to prevent the public from seeing the tremendous damaging effects of using their products. Tobacco companies were experts in misleading the public about the catastrophic damage their product did to people. I believe that similar tactics will be used to promote vaping, and it will take years before it is adequately addressed. Meanwhile there will be enormous damage done to our population, all with the goal of increased profit. This will place a heavy burden on an already strained health care system. These same vaping companies will reap enormous profits before we realize what has happened, just as we did with cigarettes.

I do not mean to minimize the problem of depression, for it is serious, and in many cases, it does require medication. There are millions of people who have benefited from drug therapy to relieve the ravages of depression and other mental conditions, but there have also been many who have been placed on these medications long term and experienced serious addiction problems as a result. An analysis of federal data shows that almost 25 million adults have been taking antidepressants for at least two years, an increase of 60 percent since 2010. For the alcoholic, however, many of those feelings that mimic depression are just another of the many forms of self-delusion that lead to yet another substance to make us feel better, or so we think.

Addiction should not be treated in a vacuum. An addicted person may need temporary drug therapy, which should be accompanied by interaction with others in recovery; it is a sign of strength when a recovering person shares with another recovering person what she is thinking to see if she is on the correct path. More often than not the advice of another person further along the path of sobriety is helpful.

IT IS ABOUT THE THINKING

"Alcoholism is a devastating, potentially fatal disease.
The primary symptom of having it is telling everyone—
including yourself—that you are not an alcoholic."
— *Herbert L. Gravitz and Julie D. Bowden,*
Recovery: A Guide for Adult Children of Alcoholics

Alcoholism has proven to be a very difficult illness to treat, for many reasons. First, it is a chronic illness that, to this point, cannot be cured. Understanding the brain and biotechnology may someday produce better solutions. Today we are utilizing drugs to curb compulsions—replacing one addictive drug with another—and in many cases we think it's necessary, because without medication the alternative is death. With the present opioid crisis and the number of deaths—70,237 from 1999 to 2017, according to the CDC—medication is needed to help prevent death due to overdose.

What gets lost very often is that this illness is not about drugs or alcohol but about how we think. Focusing on alcohol or drugs, though imperative, can cause us to miss the most daunting challenge of treating the alcoholic, because by himself, he cannot see if he is being rigorously honest. When someone relapses, it is not because he did it in consultation with another recovering person, but because he convinced himself that he could resume taking drugs or alcohol and that this time it would be different. It is only with connection to other alcoholics or addicts that he has a chance. Letting an alcoholic try to figure out when he is flawed is folly. If one is going to manage this illness, then the way he thinks is what has to be addressed.

It has been shown that by sharing our struggles with others who are afflicted with the same illness, whether cancer or alcoholism, people are able to navigate life better. I believe it is a sign of strength and not weakness to ask for help, no matter what source of power outside ourselves we connect to.

One of the core components of a 12-step program is examining oneself and making amends where needed; it has proven to be helpful for all involved. Families, colleagues, and friends are all impacted when we are trying to become a-better-version-of-ourselves. Bill Wilson and the founders of AA came up with the 12 steps to help the alcoholic to recover, which they believed was based on face-to-face interactions. They understood that two or more recovering alcoholics gathered together to help each other could overcome alcoholic thinking. Ironically, alcoholics cannot see their own thinking but can see it clearly in others. Drug therapy, although it may alleviate urges, does not produce long-term clear thinking or a plan for living a healthy life.

THE AGONY OF ALCOHOLISM

*"In my lowest moment, the only reason I didn't commit
suicide was that I knew I wouldn't be able to drink
any more if I was dead."*
— *Eric Clapton*, Clapton: The Autobiography

One of the most difficult aspects of alcoholism is its unrelenting nature. Simply stopping drinking does not relieve the alcoholic of the scourges of this illness. As we are cautioned in the AA text, the alcoholic is plagued by hundreds of forms of self-delusion, and these delusions can happen at any time, no matter how long one has been sober.

Let me describe my own experience. I was fortunate that the obsessive urge to drink was lifted early, but the thought of drinking has never left me. Those thoughts would come out of nowhere, and as with all alcoholics, I would think, "This time will be different now that I know." The first person the alcoholic lies to is himself. I have been fortunate to have many days when I am extremely grateful that I am sober. However, like all with this illness, I wake up every day an alcoholic. There have been many mornings over the years that I have awakened in an alcoholic state—that is, restless, irritable, and discontented—or have simply become alcoholic at some time during the day. It starts with just being uncomfortable and slightly irritated, looking for a target for my negative energy. Many people in recovery judge the quality of their sobriety by their driving—if they are driving aggressively, then it probably will not be a good day. What I came to realize is that on those days when I wake up in an alcoholic state, I look outside myself for someone or something to blame for the way I feel. It is almost impossible to get out of that state without first recognizing that I am in it. When I am in an alcoholic state, I am not fully aware of reality, and I am either looking for a target or trying to become a victim. In that state I am simply not aware of reality as it is; I am aware of only my reality.

What is so disconcerting to me is that I never see it coming; I don't recognize it until I am already deep in a full-blown alcoholic state. The feelings of restlessness, irritability, and discontent have a complete hold on me, and I think the cause is something outside me. It is hard for me to see the role my thinking is playing in the distortion of my reality.

When I'm in that state, the easiest mind-set for me to

adopt is that of being the victim. My first response to anything is to say no, and I am not willing to look at my own behavior. If only everybody would do what I want, then I would be OK. I am almost looking for an argument so that I can retreat to my cave, where I can wallow in self-pity and brood, meanwhile inventing new resentments against those perceived slights.

Someone told me that expectations are just premeditated resentments. So, we alcoholics must be very careful with our expectations. Being in an alcoholic state results in distorted thinking patterns. It is an awful place to be. Early on in my recovery it happened more than I would like to admit. The unfortunate recipients of our behavior are usually those closest to us—our families. I had remarried three years after getting sober, so although my wife did not experience my active alcoholic behavior, she could still bear the brunt of that behavior without me taking a drink. Fortunately for me, she learned about these alcoholic behavior patterns and helped me to recognize them earlier than I used to.

When I would get into the cave of my mind, I just could not find my way out; I could be there for a week, a month, or longer. It was painful because I could not recognize it for what it was, and so I would be stuck. Ultimately, what would get me out of it is the very last thing I would want to do: talking to someone about it. I didn't want to talk to my wife, my sponsor, or anyone at a meeting. My mind would tell me that I should not be like this, there was nothing anyone could do to help me, and it was no one's business. My alcoholism did not want me to ask for help. The longer one is in that state, the greater the chance that eventually he or she will pick up a drink to relieve the pressure. We alcoholics are all basically escapists, and we do not like to feel uncomfortable.

When I am in an alcoholic state, it is almost like a fever—I am acutely ill until finally the fever breaks and I start to recover. For me, it always ends the same way: I finally have the courage to overcome my ego and say, "I am not OK." It is usually at a seven-a.m. meeting, and then I start to come back to reality. Very often after I leave the meeting, I will call my wife and apologize yet again for my behavior. It is painful.

One time when I was in a particularly bad space, I called my sponsor, Gene, and vented to him about how my wife was the cause of my condition. He listened patiently, and when I was finished, he asked me, "How wrong is she?"

"What do you mean?" I asked.

"What percent?"

"Ninety percent."

"Then apologize for your ten percent," he said.

Of course, in reality I was 100 percent responsible for my condition, but in my state, I could not see it. Again, that apology opened the way for me to walk out of the cave. Even when I would leave the cave, my wife would be outside walking back and forth, waiting to talk about it so it would be better the next time. My response would be that it was over now, and we could move on with no discussion. How dysfunctional! That inability to have an intimate discussion has plagued me throughout my recovery.

My wife asked me recently why I continue to have the same behavior pattern, although it's not as severe as in my early years. I have tried to explain that I have a mental illness, and whether I can handle it depends on my spiritual condition. If I am spiritually fit, then I can do it; if I am not, which sometimes happens despite my best efforts, then I am doomed to repeat the same behavior. Being spiritually fit means that I am OK with what is happening in my space. No matter what is going on around me, it does not seem to bother me. When I am not fit, I am irritable, restless, and discontent. I will be defensive and disagreeable and not even be aware of it. The truth is that I have difficulty identifying my feelings and expressing them in a healthy way. I have probably been this way since childhood, and I am slowly becoming aware of the enormity of the challenge of overcoming it. Thank God Bill Wilson told us to expect "progress, not perfection." It basically took a massive intervention to get me sober, and in a way, my seven a.m. meetings are tiny interventions that allow me to see my true reality and not the distorted self-centered one my mind likes to create.

HOW INTERVENTIONS WORK

"You must do the things you think you cannot do."
— *Eleanor Roosevelt*

Although I did not appreciate my own intervention at the time, I am fortunate to have been involved in a number of them over the years. They can be very difficult and extremely emotional for all involved. Just like me, most alcoholics are highly insulted and shocked that the family would even entertain the idea of there being a problem. The leader—who should be someone outside the family, who will not be swayed by the emotion of the experience—has to be sure that everyone stays on message, because we alcoholics are great at deflecting and blaming others for our situations ("If it weren't for you, I would not be drinking."). Very often the leader will bring in the subject's child to help break down that very powerful wall of denial.

The participants may read a letter detailing a specific event to highlight the insanity of the individual's life.

Sometimes it works; sometimes it fails. I have experienced both.

I did my first intervention with a surgeon. I went to his house with his best friend, a psychiatrist, and met him in his basement. He knew something was up and did not want his wife or family in the room. He sat behind his big desk, and behind him, mounted on the wall, were about ten weapons. A few months later I took a course on how to do an intervention, and the first thing the instructor said was, "Never be in a room where the alcoholic has access to a gun." Fortunately, that night the intervention worked; the doctor was sober for more than twenty years, until he died surrounded by his loving family.

I have learned never to take credit for the success or failure of these events, because I believe that we are just messengers; something bigger than us actually makes it happen.

Over the years I have been a part of interventions that ended in failure, even with our best efforts. It might just take more work and patience before we can break through that wall of denial.

I did another intervention with an individual who also was a physician. He had been estranged from his wife and child, and when confronted with the loss of his child, he did not blink and told us that we were wasting our time because he was not going to give up alcohol. The intervention did not work, and that night we left behind a very angry man. The fact that his wife was going to divorce him and had taken his daughter away did not seem to bother him; alcohol was more important. He eventually did get into treatment, and as far as I know he is still sober. When in active addiction, the alcoholic will often do or say anything to protect his or her addiction.

THE RECKONING

"When you feel as if your whole world is falling apart,
this is actually the beginning of it being put back together,
the way it was supposed to be in the first place."
— *Christine E. Szymanski*

We are told in the book *Alcoholics Anonymous* that we have an allergy to alcohol; a small amount will trigger a reaction. Like most alcoholics, early on I seemed to have an enormous capacity for alcohol. My friends would have a few drinks and then either act drunk or get sick, yet I could drink late into the night and still be standing. For years I could drink all night without appearing to have any adverse effects. I would drink copious amounts of alcohol without getting sick or passing out. Although that is an experience many alcoholics share, we all eventually lose the ability to process alcohol. During the last years of my drinking, I started to get drunk, as my liver became less and less able to handle the alcohol.

As my father's birthday party approached in October 1986, things were closing in. A few weeks earlier one of my sisters had asked me to lunch. It was not business as usual to go to lunch with her. I didn't like the sound of it, but I agreed to go. She picked me up in front of my office and we drove ten minutes to a parking lot outside the city. She handed me a lunch bag and cut right to the chase. She asked me if I had a problem with alcohol. I answered her immediately that no, I did not, thank you very much for your concern, but I have to get right back to work.

About a week later my sister's husband, my business partner, met me after work and posed the same question. No, I did not have a problem with alcohol, but again, thank you very much. I was just having some marital problems and it was affecting my behavior. The truth was that I was by then fully addicted to alcohol and cocaine.

I saw patients on Wednesday, October 15, and that evening after work there was a cocktail party for the future governor of Pennsylvania. It was a typical fall day, not too cold, but you could feel the end of summer and the beginning of the next season. As I walked over to the hotel, I promised myself that I would not drink; I realized that everyone around me was deeply concerned about my behavior.

Walking up the steps to the front entrance of the hotel

where the fundraiser was being held, I met a friend of mine, who asked if I would like to have a drink at the bar before going out to the ballroom. My solid, heartfelt plan for a sober night vanished simply because I was asked, "Do you want a drink?" The real question should have been "Do you need a drink?" But I sure wanted one. If I am honest with myself, at that point, I also needed that drink. I was addicted. Of course, I said yes, and I had a number of vodka sodas just to feel comfortable and then mingled with the crowd for more opportunities to drink.

At about eight o'clock I left the hotel to attend my father's birthday party. I had hurriedly bought a shirt and stuck it in a brown paper bag as a present. Family and friends had gathered at my parents' home; when I got there the party was in full swing. My relationship with my father had been deteriorating over the years due to my drinking. The more I drank, the more strain there was. During that time my drinking had caused me to become angrier. Anger, which is really just fear, is one of the few emotions that an active alcoholic seems to show consistently. It is used to protect his or her addiction. If we can just keep everybody on edge, then they won't confront us about our behavior, and we can continue on the path of self-destruction.

Although I do not know exactly what was said at the party, I do know that I was blaming everyone for my problems and that I was filled with resentment. I was pointing my finger at my father, and I remember what he said to me. He handed my gift back and said he did not want it. He told me to stop talking. He said, "Stop pointing the finger at me and look at the three pointing back at you." Of course, I was insulted and stormed out of the house, returning to the city to find some solace with my friends at one of the bars I frequented. I drank with two of my drinking friends and complained bitterly about my father, eventually moving on to other, more important national problems and coming up with solutions. At one point they suggested that I run for Congress.

My life was a mess. I was not faithful to my first wife, I was an absentee father, and I was an impaired professional. The tragedy continued the next day, on my son's birthday, when I put my clothes in two leaf-and-lawn bags and moved into a motel not far from my home. I look back at that day and realize just how ill I had become. I remember holding the two bags over my shoulders. The plastic drawstrings were tight, choking off the circulation in my fingers. I ignored that and acted like it was normal for me to leave the house dressed in a sport coat and tie carrying my belongings in trash bags, with no plan or idea what was next. I knew I was in trouble, but the severity of my situation just would not register. As with all alcoholics, this was a defense mechanism: If I ignore the situation, it doesn't exist. That is why outing yourself at an AA meeting is so important—it ensures that you can no longer ignore the reality that you have avoided.

The next night, two of my brothers asked me to meet with them so that I could hear their concerns, and I agreed. I argued with them that my problems were due to my wife and my work. They did not accept my arguments and kept going back to my drinking, but I resisted. For two hours they tried to get me to see my own behavior. I finally agreed to meet on Monday with a friend of the family who worked at Marworth Treatment Center, just a few miles from my home.

I did not drink that Friday, Saturday, or Sunday. I stayed in a poorly furnished motel room by myself, contemplating whether I should keep the meeting or flee to Mexico.

Monday morning, I dressed in a camel hair coat, gray slacks, white shirt, and tie to look my best. I was sweating, my hands were shaking, I did not feel well, and my complexion was a shade of gray.

When I got to Marworth, I was led to the hospital wing

for an intake evaluation and questioned about my history. Of course, I lied and minimized, hoping that the intake team would realize it was all a big mistake. Turns out even my minimized version of my addiction qualified for treatment. In the meantime, they asked for my keys. I pleaded my case, but no one bought it; I was not leaving. My run for Congress was over, the shortest political career on record. My new life was about to begin, even though I was unaware of it.

THE PARADOX OF THE ALCOHOLIC

*"I have absolutely no pleasure in the stimulants in which I
sometimes so madly indulge. It has not been in the pursuit of
pleasure that I have periled life and reputation and reason.
It has been the desperate attempt to escape from torturing
memories, from a sense of insupportable loneliness and a
dread of some strange impending doom."*
— *Edgar Allan Poe*

Austin Ripley, the founder of Guest House, a rehabilitation center for Catholic clergy diagnosed with addiction,
wrote the following, which I think sums up an alcoholic
fairly well:

> The alcoholic, of course, is many things, as we all know.
> He is the world's supreme paradox. He drinks not be-
> cause he would, but because he must. He does not drink
> for pleasure; he drinks to pain, yet he drinks. He will
> mortgage the wealth of the future to pay off the debts of
> the past so that he may drink up the non-existent present.
>
> He is the only one in nature, I think, who seeks stim-
> ulation in a sedative, only to find it acts upon his nerves

as excited misery. He seeks to inflate his puny little ego in the provocative wine of Bacchus and succeeds in shriveling his soul in the bitter gall of remorse.

He escapes desperately to free himself from the facts of reality and runs headlong into the prison of fantasy. Success is just as fatal as failure to the alcoholic. He will drink with exhilaration to success and to sadness and misfortune. He drinks to get high in the evening, knowing how low he will be in the morning.

When the alcoholic smilingly gets to the first drink he can get, he is transported to heaven and when he is unable to get the last drink he can pour, he is transported to hell. The alcoholic, like most people, thrills to the beauty of life, and then how frequently he seeks the ugliness of existence. When he is sober, he craves to be drunk. When he is drunk, he prays to be sober. Such is the weird paradox of the alcoholic; that the only way in which he can feel better is to drink that which makes him feel worse.

He starts out on his drinking, no matter who he is, with all the dignity of a king, and winds up his drinking like a clown. So, he goes his incredible incomprehensible, paradoxical way, leaving in his wake human wreckage, that which he does cherish most. Down the road of alcoholic oblivion, he stumbles and staggers, until he either finds himself at the door of A.A. or death intervenes.

HONESTY

"Being honest may not get you a lot of friends
but it'll always get you the right ones.
— John Lennon

As I've mentioned, the first person the alcoholic has to
lie to is herself. We alcoholics drink great quantities on a
routine basis. However, if you ask an alcoholic how much
she drank, she will almost always minimize the amount.
She had "a couple" or "a few" or maybe even "a few too
many," but it's never the truth. The truth would be too
much to bear or to explain away. We must protect our
addiction, even from ourselves. A normally thinking person is horrified by even the possibility of ingesting the
amount of alcohol that the alcoholic will do on a routine
basis and then justify to herself. This lack of honesty is
crucial to the continued progression of the illness. The
ability to rationalize one's behavior is essential. So, when
we get sober, that habit of being dishonest has to be elim-
inated. If it returns, then we first start to lie to ourselves,

and before we know it, we somehow can justify, with what seems like logic, picking up a drink or a drug.

I remember one fellow saying at a meeting that he was honest because when he and his partner would break in and steal drugs from the pharmacy, he would be certain to divide the number of pills right down the middle. That ability to self-delude is so powerful that it can be changed only when the alcoholic shares with another recovering person what he is thinking. Only then does clarity of thought start to take hold. This sharing with others just how we think helps to guard us and helps us to develop a new way of thinking. The alcoholic must guard against this throughout his recovery because the tendency to lie is always there.

Bill Wilson and his colleagues knew this was a problem for us, so when they wrote the book the adjective they used before the word *honesty* was *rigorous*, not *indulgent* or *lax*. This rigorous honesty must be in place at all times, because one lie leads to another and before you know it, you are on the slippery slope of relapse.

THE BRAIN DISORDER

"Alcohol ruined me financially and morally,
broke my heart and the hearts of too many others. Even
though it did this to me and it almost killed me, and I haven't
touched a drop of it in seventeen years, sometimes I wonder if
I could get away with drinking some now. I totally subscribe
to the notion that alcoholism is a mental illness because
thinking like that is clearly insane."
— Craig Ferguson

Recently I read in *Scientific American* that addiction is "a chronic brain disorder, a treatable medical condition involving changes to circuits involved in reward, stress, and self-control."[11] The article, titled "What Does It Mean When We Call Addiction a Brain Disorder?" by Nora Volkow, goes on to state that the medical model of addiction as a brain disorder or disease has vocal critics. Some claim that viewing addiction this way minimizes its important social and environmental causes, as though considering addiction a disorder of the brain circuits means social stressors such as loneliness, poverty, violence, and other psychological environmental factors do not play an important role. In fact, the dominant theoretical framework in addiction science today is the biopsychosocial framework, which recognizes the complex interaction between biology, behavior, and environment. Volkow goes on to state that "medications cannot take the place of an individual's willpower, but . . . they have been shown in study after study to reduce illicit drug use and its consequences."[12] Medications save lives, but they are not the answer to long-term sobriety for most. In conclusion, Volkow writes:

Addiction is indeed many things—a maladaptive response to environmental stressors, a development disorder, a disorder caused by dysregulation of brain circuits, and yes, a learned behavior. We will never be able to address addiction without being able to talk about and address the myriad factors that contribute to it—biological, psychological, behavioral, societal, economic, etc. But viewing it as a treatable medical problem from which people can and do recover is crucial for enabling a public health–focused response that ensures access to effective treatments and lessens the stigma surrounding a condition that afflicts nearly 10 percent of Americans at some point in their lives.[13]

I agree with much of what Volkow points out and believe we are in a period of history when pharmaceutical companies are looking for drugs to treat addiction. I am also in favor of any treatment, drug or otherwise, that increases the chances of success, but I am skeptical of long-term medication as the answer to addiction.

The treatment of alcoholism has been difficult because it is a physical, mental, and spiritual illness. By "spiritual," I do not in any way mean religious. I mean it in the context that all of us have a spirit. The idea that we're all just part of a system of biochemical reactions within the brain seems like only half the story of human existence. Science cannot and will not look at any notion of spirit because it cannot be seen or measured, but many believe that each of us has a spiritual nature.

There are many critics of the 12-step program because it is seen as a Christian program and therefore religious. I can certainly appreciate those views; it was one of the issues I struggled with early in my recovery. Because of this inclusion of the spiritual as part of AA, there are great prejudices against the program, and many opt out because of what they perceive as a God issue, or because they believe AA is promoting Christianity. There have been times over the years when people in AA have attempted to evangelize me, and I have to respect the path they have chosen and not judge them. I certainly have struggled with it and at times continue to do so. However, I have come to understand just how important spirituality is to recovery. Although I have heard people talk about their "personal savior," or their God, I have never felt pressure to accept anyone else's source of power.

The book *Alcoholics Anonymous* was written without the scientific knowledge of today. The early pioneers of AA did realize, however, that alcoholism is a physical, mental, and spiritual malady, for they stressed the importance of addressing all three of these issues for any possibility of success. Many called it the three-legged stool. We cannot just stop drinking; we have to address our thinking. In the depths of alcoholism, most of us neglect our health and have terrible eating habits and erratic sleeping patterns. Along with the mental and physical damage, our spirit is probably giving off very negative energy. In order for us to recover, all three of these areas of our lives have to be addressed, and we must eventually realize that our dependence on some higher power is also an important part of our recovery. All three legs of this stool must be treated, or the seat will not hold.

There was a tremendous Christian influence on the

authors of the AA text. However, they were well aware that this influence would be a problem. In their wisdom, they declared that it did not have to be God in the religious sense; it would instead be a power greater than we are. These are not just Christian principles, but universal ideas of connection and diminished ego. That higher power could be another person, a group of people, or the universe—anything but the addict him- or herself. There are those who bristle at this as though it is a sign of weakness, believing that each person is perfectly capable, with the correct information, to overcome his or her addiction. Although this may be true for some, I believe it is a sign of strength when one reaches out for help, and I have witnessed the power of such action. However, it is still a significant issue for many who cannot accept the AA program because they associate it with religion.

Bill Wilson just wanted alcoholics to admit that there was some power greater than themselves that they could rely on. In my case, early in my sobriety, I drew strength from nature. Consider that the estimated diameter of the universe is 93 billion light years, and light travels at 186,282 miles per second. This is virtually impossible for our human brains to comprehend in any relative sense. The sheer power of the natural world and the magnitude of its spirit showed me grace. By tapping into nature, I was able to recognize a power greater than myself and achieve ego deflation. I realized that I was just a minuscule part of an unbelievable system and that I had to be grateful to have experienced it, if only for a brief time in the fabric of this amazing universe.

Instead of becoming more self-sufficient, I experienced a healthy sense of humility and was more willing to listen to others. That willingness to open my mind to the possibility that there truly is some greater power made me more open to the world of spirit. I would not be here if it were not for the grace of something larger than me.

Over the years I've gained a deeper appreciation for the wisdom of the founders of AA and how effective this program can be if it is followed as directed. The problem is that when it is not followed as directed, the results are often relapse and possibly even death. As we have all heard at one time, it is a simple program for complicated people.

There are some misconceptions about AA. Some think that alcoholics just sit around and drink coffee, smoke cigarettes, and tell war stories. Today the vast majority of meetings are nonsmoking. There is still plenty of coffee and certainly we share our experiences. However, these experiences are shared only so that we can relate to each other. Drinking and using drugs is the problem, and the meetings are about solutions.

Most meetings start with the alcoholic telling a little about him or herself, and then the chairperson will ask for a topic. That topic could be anything—anger, fear, resentment, difficulty with life as it presents. The purpose is for the person sharing to do so openly and honestly, and then to ask for help. Remember that most often the alcoholic has difficulty seeing himself. This openness gives the person an opportunity to become more self-aware by listening to the experience of others. That self-awareness is carried out the door and the alcoholic has a reasonable chance of remaining sober for another twenty-four hours.

MORE

"The mother of excess is not joy but joylessness."
— *Friedrich Nietzsche*, Human, All Too Human:
A Book for Free Spirits

Addiction is about more. More alcohol, more drugs, more sex, more gambling, more porn, more sports, more of whatever it is that we are addicted to. For the alcoholic the thought would be "Will there be enough when I start to drink?" At a function, will there be enough alcohol, or will it run out? In a bar, can I drink enough before it closes? At home, do I have enough, or will I run out? Unfortunately, there is never enough.

After rehab, I went back home to attempt to save my marriage to my first wife. There was a double-door pantry off the kitchen where I stashed my "supply." There had been bottles of all sorts of liquor in case of war or the end of the world. I opened the door, and the pantry was bare. I asked my wife what had happened to all the bottles. She told me that she had poured them out. Now, I had just left the rehabilitation center, and I was furious. How could she have done that! I was still holding on, and I could not see it. What a terrible waste of my precious supply, or so I thought. That difficult time in early recovery eventually resulted in the failure of my marriage, which was my fault, even though I could not see it at that time. I have learned that clarity of thinking does not return in early recovery. Many think it can take up to five years before we are able to think clearly.

I had a friend with a dual addiction of alcohol and gambling. He had lost everything at one point—his house, his pension plan, and all of his savings. He took his eight-year-old son to Atlantic City, New Jersey, under the guise of spending more time with him. While he was downstairs in the casino, he left his son in the hotel room with a milkshake from room service. He proceeded to gamble away thousands of dollars, and when he came back to the room to discover his son had drunk only half of the milk shake, he found himself screaming at his child for being wasteful.

Another man told me how he and his wife had gone out to a bar and he'd spent $150 on drinks. When they returned home and were getting ready for bed, his wife brushed her teeth and then discarded the toothpaste tube. He screamed at her for wasting toothpaste and demanded that she get him a set of pliers so that he could prove that there were two more dabs in the tube.

It was only upon reflection that both of these men could see their need for more; in the midst of their self-centered behavior, neither could see his own selfishness.

Because the need for more is always present, the addict is in a constant state of distraction. A friend of mine once said he had only one problem with cocaine: running out. We are always preparing to use, actually using, or recovering from using, which means there is never enough time for the important matters of life, like our families, our health, and our jobs. We are impaired at all levels.

The other side of this need for more is fear. If there is not enough, the addict will experience fear; it will be a constant companion. As a result, the addict will never be able to be present in the moment, because he or she will be in a continuous state of worry. How exhausting.

NO ONE GOES TO REHAB ON A GOOD DAY

*"I hated every minute of training, but I said, 'Don't quit.
Suffer now and live the rest of your life as a champion.'"*
— *Muhammad Ali*

When not feeling well, most people will make an appointment with their doctor to find out what may be wrong. Not the alcoholic. Invariably we are the last to know about, admit, or address our serious illness.

There is an old saying that it takes "a nudge, a grudge, or a judge" to get us to think about the possibility that there is something wrong with us. It is truly amazing just how powerful addiction is, and how we want to hold on to it and justify it no matter what damage it has done, both physical and emotional.

Even when you are in an institution, as I was, it sometimes can take days or weeks to break through the wall of denial. In some cases that wall is never breached. As the AA book tells us, "There are those too who are constitutionally incapable of being honest with themselves. It does seem that those who have the capacity to be honest with themselves have a chance to recover if they are willing to follow the simple program of recovery."[14]

CUNNING, BAFFLING, AND POWERFUL

*"The idea that somehow, someday he will control
and enjoy his drinking is the great obsession of
every abnormal drinker."*
— Alcoholics Anonymous

Who would ever want to have the illness of alcoholism? I once asked a group of physicians and other health care professionals who were in treatment, "If you had a choice of these life-threatening illnesses—alcoholism, diabetes, cancer, dementia, or heart disease—which would you choose?" There was silence. They were debating in their minds how they could justify hanging on to their alcoholism. Of the five, alcoholism has the least-serious side effects when the patient is in recovery. And yet the alcoholic pauses because we desperately want to be able to drink.

One of the most important paragraphs in *Alcoholics Anonymous* is the following: Most of us have been unwilling to admit we were real Alcoholics. No person likes to think he is bodily and mentally different from his fellows. Therefore, it is not surprising that our drinking careers have been characterized by countless vain attempts to prove we could drink like other people. The idea that somehow, someday he will control and enjoy his drinking is the great obsession of every abnormal drinker. The persistence of this illusion is astonishing. Many pursue it to the gates of insanity or death.[15]

I am reminded of a story that the late Sandy B., one of the great AA speakers, used to tell. It goes like this. The alcoholic's life is like being on a game show. The alcoholic is onstage with the game show host, who says to him, "There are two doors in front of you. Behind one door is a reasonably happy life, and behind the other is an alcoholic death. Which door do you choose? The alcoholic says, "Just how bad is an alcoholic death?" When in active addiction, the alcoholic's body cannot process alcohol or drugs, and his mind cannot process reality.

When confronted with the reality of his life, the alcoholic thinks, "Just please don't tell me I have to stop drinking." I can remember clearly, as if it happened yesterday, my intake interview at Marworth Treatment Center. I was in the office of Dr. Nick Colangelo, the director; with him was Dr. Bruce Branin, the chief medical officer. They were asking about my drinking and drug use.

Of course, I lied and presented a sanitized version of my history, minimizing my substance use. They knew I was lying, because all alcoholics lie when confronted with the truth of their lives. I was willing to say and do anything to protect my addiction. After my interview, I was told that I would be staying and that my family did not want me back until I confronted myself and did something about it.

That night, back in my room, I wept out of despair. It was probably the first time I had shed a tear since I was a child. Growing up, we were told to "knock it off" if we cried, so I learned to stuff my feelings. If I was overwhelmed and could not hold back my emotions, I was admonished to stop it or "I will give you something to cry for." That night all my emotions boiled over, and I just could not keep them inside, so I wept until I could weep no more. I thought my life was over, that I would never again be able to have fun. There would be no release from the pressures of living. I was being sentenced to a life of doom and gloom. My thinking was so distorted, my feelings so suppressed that I was unable to see the future. How wrong I was.

DENIAL

"I protect myself by refusing to know myself."
— *Floriano Martins*

Denial is the most powerful aspect of addiction. It's the reason so many do not recover and eventually die from this disease. All humans use denial in some way to avoid reality. When we are told that we have a fatal illness, the first thing the human brain does is insist that it is not so. It must be a mistake, a misdiagnosis, anything but the truth. It is only upon reflection that we are able to eventually accept the truth of our situation.

For alcoholics, denial usually starts early in a pattern of self-deception. When confronted with their drug or alcohol abuse, they minimize or deny. When told that they have a problem, they deflect, lie, or blame others for their situation. Finally, when all else fails, the addict will blame forces beyond his or her control. A common refrain is, "If you had to live with this person, you would drink too."

When I first entered the rehab facility, I was certain sending me there had been a mistake, an overreaction.

I was convinced that after an evaluation the treatment team would realize their mistake and release me. At worst they may say that I drank too much, but that I could easily change now that I knew the problems I had caused. As history has taught me, I was completely unaware of the truth of my life.

My sponsor once told me that if he had been given a lie detector test on the way to the rehab facility and asked if he were an alcoholic, he would have said no, and he is certain he would have passed. He had convinced himself that he was just a heavy drinker, not an alcoholic. He just needed to let off steam periodically to relieve the stress of his job; he could not possibly be an alcoholic.

On his intake the physician took copious notes. At one point during the interview, the doctor excused himself to attend to another matter, and when he left, my sponsor saw the notepad and was able to read the first sentence, even though it was upside down. "The patient is a 35-year-old white male who suffers from chronic alcoholism." It was the first time that his wall of denial crumbled just enough for him to recognize the reality of his life.

Just about every patient at their intake invariably lies about their drinking or usage. The thought of not drinking or using drugs is just too overwhelming. One of my friends told me that every morning he would check to see if the whites of his eyes were yellow, and if they were, he would quit, but not until then.

One of my aunts, who despite many attempts could not get sober, asked me as she lay in her hospital bed dying from esophageal varices and organ failure, "Why is this happening to me?" I had been sober for about eight years at that point, and I was angry with her because she refused to see the reality of her situation. Even on her deathbed she could not accept that her drinking was the reason she was dying. *Tell me something else; don't tell me I am an alcoholic.* I still did not fully appreciate the power of alcoholism in late-stage addiction. She, like my other alcoholic aunt, died at the age of fifty-four. These were my mother's sisters; the whole family was riddled with alcoholism. Fortunately for me, my mother was spared, but like my aunts, I had the same illness. To this day, that scene in the hospital room is such a powerful memory for me, because it was the reality of what this illness is capable of doing if it's not addressed.

So, when an alcoholic is put into a rehab facility, the first thing the counselors have to do is try to break through the wall of denial. It is difficult because the alcoholic is well versed in deflection. This denial has to be breached for the alcoholic or addict to have any chance of recovery.

About a month after I left the rehab one of my brothers, who is not an alcoholic, said to me, "You are so fortunate to have been in rehab."

I replied, "You must be kidding."

He said, "You had the opportunity to step out of your life and find out who you are."

That conversation has always stayed with me. My brother would have welcomed the opportunity to learn more about himself. I was the opposite; I could not bear to look deep into my being and learn the truth about myself. Today is different. Over time I have become more willing to listen without reacting, but that underlying sensitivity remains, and I try to be aware of it.

EMOTION, OR THE LACK OF IT

"That's all drugs and alcohol do,
they cut off your emotions in the end."
— Ringo Starr

One of the most perplexing characteristics about alcoholics and addicts is their difficulty in feeling or expressing emotion. The ones they seem most capable of exhibiting are fear and anger. These two emotions are hardwired; they have been with humans since the beginning of time in order to help us survive in a very dangerous world when our species first appeared on earth. The rest of the emotions evolved as humans evolved. The problem of the alcoholic is that we use these two emotions to protect our addictions and in some ways are never able to evolve into complete beings. For the alcoholic anger and fear are wrapped up in their illness. The loss of an addictive substance is just too overwhelming, and any attempt to give it up can result in a highly charged angry response.

Perhaps it is because of some childhood trauma or the loss of the ability to emote after one starts to drink or use.

There may be many reasons for this inability to feel. The use of alcohol and drugs very often takes down that wall and then addict can seem to express feelings, although most often they are negative feelings. As soon as they are no longer under the influence the wall goes back up. I suspect that it is because all alcoholics and addicts share the character defect of self-centeredness. We are told that self-centeredness is the root of all our problems. If we are self-centered, we can't possibly have an objective view of ourselves, and so we hide behind the veil of our selfishness, thinking only about ourselves, how and when we can escape that uncomfortable world, and take care of our own needs.

Others have pointed out to me that at times I appear to be standing on the sidelines of life, observing what is going on around me but not participating. This is probably due to an inability to connect with others, which means I am unable to feel or share emotions.

I listened to a woman share that as a child she and her siblings were not allowed to cry for any reason. Some years later, when she was a young adult, her father died. On the way to the church her mother said to her, "I hope no one cries at the funeral." The daughter was shocked and said, "But Mom, Dad just died." How powerful that early training was and how profound the effect on the ability of the family to express emotions.

Very often in rehabilitation centers patients are shown pictures of faces expressing emotion—happy, sad, angry, fearful, and so on—to try to get the alcoholic to identify what they are feeling. For some it can be a very difficult exercise.

Recently a woman I know shared at a meeting that after about three years of being sober she felt very sad. At first, she did not recognize the feeling, then she felt guilty for being sad. She was just not accustomed to feeling, and for days she struggled with an emotion that seemed so foreign to her. In speaking about it—in connecting with other people—she was able to recognize that what she was feeling was perfectly normal.

Very often those feelings of anger and fear lurk just below the surface, and they can show themselves at the most inopportune time. Like most alcoholics, I have been guilty of this, reacting instead of responding to whatever difficult situation I was facing. Time has reduced the frequency of those incidents, but I can still act inappropriately in the face of fear and anger. This is why there is a specific step requiring us to apologize promptly when we act inappropriately. Very often we are convinced that we are justified, until we explain the situation to another alcoholic and find out that our perception may not be accurate. Most often we are not justified, and even if we are, we must recognize our part, no matter how big or small.

We cannot learn to recognize emotions by taking methadone or buprenorphine. Instead, like with my friend who was sad, we need a human connection to help us understand what we are feeling and then process that emotion.

To succeed for long term recovery the one emotion the alcoholic must work to recognize is gratitude. We must be grateful for what we have and to acknowledge that leaving a life of chaos and instability is in itself worthy of a deep sense of gratitude. This specific emotion is linked to well-being and better health, the benefits of which are instrumental to staying on the path to contentment. Certainly, when one starts down the path of sobriety there is an improvement in one's health and well-being.

Those initial feelings have to be nurtured and constantly worked on if one is to remain sober. Gratitude is a useful answer to our long-term health. In order to maintain that gratitude, we must be in reality, not our own distorted version of it. By ourselves we very often do not recognize how truly fortunate we are to be in recovery. When we listen to the experiences of others, we can start to recognize that the problems we are facing are most often short term or if serious can be addressed with the help of others. This is why the human connection is so important for recovering people. We need others to first help us to see reality and then to direct us to the proper response to whatever situation is troubling us.

I certainly have struggled to identify my own emotions; it's something I continue to work on, and I still sometimes fall very short. The only thing that has saved me thus far is that I am enormously grateful that I am sober. Without that I would be doomed.

THE GREATEST PARADOX

"Alcohol is a perfect solvent; it dissolves marriages, families, and careers."
— *Unknown*

I suppose all humans have some difficulty seeing themselves. Many people are healthy enough to pursue therapy just for the opportunity to get a clearer view of themselves by sharing with a trained professional. As I mentioned, alcoholics and addicts simply cannot see themselves, and for the most part they are unwilling to allow anyone to help them. What is interesting is that they can clearly see other recovering people and register whether they are being honest with themselves. However, left on their own in an alcoholic state, they cannot see the truth of their own lives.

When confronted with their behavior, most alcoholics are defensive, denying what the person confronting them sees; or they quickly become the victim. It can be very difficult to communicate with someone who is in this alcoholic state.

One Saturday morning my friend Tom said, "I had a terrible argument with my wife this morning." He paused and followed up with, "The only problem is that she hadn't woken up yet."

Tom woke up alcoholic and unable to see himself. He was irritable, restless, and discontented, looking for a target outside himself; as usual, it's a family member who receives the most blowback from such bad emotional behavior.

Tom left the house before his wife woke, took his state of mind to a meeting, and spoke about it. While describing his condition and listening to others who had been in the same situation, he realized that he was in his false reality. He went home after the meeting and told his wife he loved her and appreciated that she stood by him even though he exhibited bizarre and inexplicable behavior at times.

This inability to see ourselves if we are not exposed to other recovering people can eventually lead down the path to relapse. As we know, alcoholism is a thinking disorder, and that disordered thinking is what gets us into trouble. Continually exposing our distorted thinking is what saves us from ourselves.

Most family members know nothing about recovery, but they know that when the alcoholic in their life attends meetings, they return home in a better mental state.

DIABETES, HYPERTENSION, AND ALCOHOLISM HAVE MUCH IN COMMON

"Alcoholism is a devastating, potentially fatal disease.
The primary symptom of having it is telling everyone—
including yourself—that you are not an alcoholic."
— Herbert L. Gravitz & Julie D. Bowden

Diabetes may be the most understood of all human illnesses. With proper treatment and a change in diet, most diabetic patients can live long and relatively healthy lives, yet many do not take their medication as directed or make the necessary modifications to their diet, suffering serious complications as a result. Not only do they continue to eat foods that make their illness worse, but on average, 50 percent of new medication users fail to consume at least 80 percent of prescribed doses during their first year of therapy.

Similarly, despite increased awareness, patients with hypertension often fail to take their medication as directed, which results in an increased risk of coronary and cardiovascular events.

Alcoholics are no different. With all three illnesses, the patients are diagnosed, and treatment protocols given. In the case of the first two, medications are prescribed. The patient starts taking them, and very often stops as soon as she starts to feel better, suffering physical consequences that can lead to disability or death if she doesn't resume her medication.

As I've mentioned, I spoke to a drug rep who works with physicians who treat diabetics, and she shocked me when she told me that many of her doctors find it challenging and frustrating to work with diabetic patients. When I asked her why, she said it was because many don't follow directions, which eventually results in serious complications that need to be addressed. A review of the literature found treatment adherence rates among diabetics between 36 and 93 percent. These are general adherence rates, and there are many diabetics who do follow their physician's directions and lead long, reasonably healthy lives. In the case of alcoholism, the patient is given 12 steps to follow and encouraged to go to meetings, every day if necessary. If the alcoholic adheres to this plan, he has a very good chance of recovery. In many cases as soon as he feels better, he stops following directions and within a short period of time returns to drinking.

There are those who argue that AA does not work. I disagree. It works as well as treatment for diabetes and hypertension—if the patient follows directions. The real problem is complacency, and that applies to any chronic illness.

THE OPIOID TRAGEDY

"The opioid epidemic has been described as," one of the greatest mistakes in modern medicine." But calling it a mistake is a generous rewriting of the history of greed, corruption and indifference that pushed the US into consuming 80 percent of the opioid painkillers."
— *Chris McGreal*

Most problems with addictive drugs such as heroin start in the street. The opioid crisis began on the street, and now the companies who manufacture the drugs have spread it from the street into the home. Pharmaceutical companies, the FDA, and our medical communities fuel the opioid addiction problem. The United States accounts for 6 percent of the world's population but consumes 80 percent of its pharmaceuticals.

When opioids were first introduced by the pharmaceutical industry, we were assured that they were not addictive. It has been reported that Purdue Pharma knew about significant abuse of OxyContin in the first year after the drug was introduced in 1996 and concealed that information. The drug maker continued to market Oxy-Contin as less likely to lead to abuse and addiction.

When Opana, a powerful opioid, was first introduced, the FDA advisory committee voted 14 to 1 against introducing the drug to the public. Because of the power of lobbying, it was successfully released for use to an unsuspecting public. Endo International removed Opana from the market in 2017 because of the terrible addiction problem it caused.

Recently the FDA approved an opioid called Dsuvia. The tablet dissolves under the tongue to give fast pain relief from extreme trauma. It was approved for use only in supervised settings, such as a hospital. The drug contains thirty micrograms of a synthetic opioid known as sufentanil, which is five to ten times more powerful than fentanyl and a thousand times more potent than morphine. Many experts argued against approval by the FDA, including the chair of its own advisory committee on opioids. The FDA voted 10 to 3 to approve Dsuvia.

Early on in this national crisis, physicians and dentists were advised to prescribe opioids without proper knowledge of the risk of addiction, and prescriptions were written for too many pills and refilled too often. Some unscrupulous doctors became very wealthy writing scripts for patients without even performing any exams.

The drug companies produced more pills than were ever needed as an addiction disaster was created throughout the United States. For example, according to a congressional committee investigating the opioid crisis, over the past decade out-of-state drug companies shipped 20.8 million prescription painkillers to two pharmacies four blocks apart in a West Virginia town with a population of 2,900. This is just one example of many abuses.

This disaster is finally being addressed as states are suing the pharmaceutical companies and going after unscrupulous providers to stem the flow of opioids. There are now more efforts to treat the enormous number of victims of this tragedy.

ALCOHOL VERSUS OPIOIDS

"I'm very serious about no alcohol, no drugs.
Life is too beautiful."
— Jim Carrey

According to the National Institute on Alcohol Abuse and Alcoholism, an estimated 88,000 (approximately 62,000 men and 26,000 women) died from alcohol-related causes in 2017, while more than 72,000 died from opioid abuse.

Outside of traffic fatalities, falls, and homicides, death due to alcoholism is a long, slow progression, ultimately caused by gastric bleeds, esophageal varices, cirrhosis, diabetes, cardiac events, stroke, or cancer. Many alcohol-related deaths occur later in life.

The opposite is true for opioids. Most of the deaths caused by these potent drugs occur when the addict is young, or soon after addiction begins. Because they are so young, many cannot accept the possibility of death; it simply does not enter their mind.

I am told by those involved with the treatment of alcoholics and addicts that treating opioid addicts is much more difficult than treating alcoholics. Opioid addicts are more resistant, stronger in their denial, and more apt to check themselves out of treatment against medical advice. Because they are typically younger, their deaths seem to be much more tragic.

MY MIND IS OUT TO GET ME

"Fall seven times, stand up eight."
– Japanese proverb

At a seven-a.m. meeting my friend Clyde said something that I had never heard before: "My mind is out to get me." I was struck by this because I realized just how true it was, and that without AA and a sponsor I would not be able to understand just how flawed my thinking was. This is not about dependence; it is about awareness.

I learned, as most recovering alcoholics do, that it was not my drinking that led to my fall but my thinking. What seemed like a good idea every day led me down a path of self-destructive behavior. For every incident I had, I had an answer or excuse. Everything made perfect sense to me, yet my family found it necessary to force me into a rehabilitation hospital. When I left the facility, I still had the same distorted thinking. My mind told me that the experience was very nice but a little bit overdone. All I needed to do was be aware of my thinking and then I could successfully live my new life on my own, without the interference of these nice people.

Fortunately for me, the day I was released from the rehabilitation center the director sat me down with my counselors and told me the gentleman sitting across the table from me was going to be my sponsor. His name was Gene M.; he was a former lieutenant colonel in the US Marines and a former CBS executive. Looking back, I realize that I probably would not have made it to this point in my life without his wisdom and guidance. He insisted that I call him every day, which I did for a number of years. He never told me what to do; he just suggested that I might do something different than what I thought was the correct course. Invariably his ideas were better than mine.

Early on I needed help with lots of decisions. I was going through a divorce, which was the result of my alcoholism, and I was fragile. Where should I live? Could I go into a bar or restaurant? Could I go to a wedding? They seemed like simple decisions, but I would obsess about them because I was filled with fear about whether I was making the right choice. Almost always, my sponsor would break every decision down to one question: What's your motive? I'd never given that a thought, but he would guide me until it became clear which path I should take.

What I find most interesting is that although I was sober, there were many occasions when my first thought was self-destructive. Because I had that strong figure in my early recovery, I eventually found it easy to call someone when I was not sure if I was making the right decision. I'd run whatever I was thinking by that person and ask him what he thought. More times than not I followed the direction given by another recovering alcoholic rather than my own.

At a recent meeting, a member who has been sober for five years said that he experienced his mother's death drunk and that he drank all throughout her passing and funeral. He wondered out loud what it would take for him to drink again and said he had been thinking about it for a few weeks. Just what kind of tragedy would give him license to drink again? He then told us that on the previous Saturday he had been home alone all day, and after he finished watching a football game the thought came to him that this would be a perfect time to have a beer. It made him realize that it wasn't the gravity of a situation that would give him permission to drink—he was an alcoholic, and his mind would always be searching for permission, in good situations and in bad.

Like all alcoholics, I drank when it was sunny and when it was raining, when we won and when we lost, when I was happy and when I was sad. I drank because I was an alcoholic, not because of good or bad situations.

Most of my thoughts are about myself and my own needs. What I have learned is that I am at my best when I'm willing to communicate, when I'm willing to do something for someone else and put his or her needs ahead of mine. That is easy to put on paper, but because my basic nature is self-centered, I have to be fully present and aware, or I will make the wrong choice. As Matthew Kelly, the author of more than twenty books, has taught me, all day every day I am given choices, those that will make me a-better-version-of-myself and those that will make me a diminished version. Only clarity of thought enables me to see when my mind is out to get me.

ANGER AND FEAR

"Fear is the path to the dark side. Fear leads to anger.
Anger leads to hate. Hate leads to suffering."
— *George Lucas via the character Yoda*

When I first became sober, I moved out of my house; alcoholism had destroyed my marriage beyond repair. I rented an apartment and set out to attend ninety meetings in ninety days. I was filled with anger, or what I thought was anger. For almost two years little things would set me off. I may not have shown it, but inside I was in a rage most of the time. Things were just not going my way, and I did not like it.

A long-term recovering friend, Vince, told me that early in recovery, many alcoholics have only two emotions, rage and suppressed rage. It took some time, but after those two years I started to realize I was just afraid—afraid I could not drink, afraid I could not control my life, afraid the future was going to be bleak, afraid of what other people thought. I was just plain afraid, and it took me some time to see it and understand it. Learning how to express those thoughts and to listen to others who had the same thought patterns was the key to relieving them. It's not that I don't still have fears; it's that now most of the time I can recognize that they are not based in reality.

I finally learned that I was not able to live in the moment. I was either full of regret for the past or worried about the future. Today is different. With practice and mindfulness, I am able to be present, to be living fully in what is happening in this moment. I cannot do it all the time, but it is now what I strive for. There are even times when I will stop what I am doing and just stand up and realize that I am totally present in that moment. It can be fleeting, and I can return to those feelings of dread and uncertainty. But there are now days when I wake and am filled with gratitude for where I am in my life.

There are other days when I wake in an alcoholic state, worrying about the future and what it might bring. The difference is that now I can see it; I can do things to get out of the irritable, restless, discontented state that is so normal for an alcoholic.

The first and most difficult thing I must do is become aware that I am in an alcoholic frame of mind. Most of the time I cannot see it; I think it's a person or circumstance that is causing me angst. Second, I must tell someone that I am not OK. That sounds easy, but when I am in this zone, the last thing I want to do is tell another person. It is only after I become aware of my insanity that I can start to return to actual reality, not my reality.

By exposing my thoughts, I am able to realize the anger is just fear. This was a very important lesson I learned on the path of recovery. AA meetings change my view of everything in my day because I am able to recognize my own insanity.

Meetings are so vital to one's mental health and dispelling anger and fear. Remember that the alcoholic lives most of the day in his or her own mind, and that mind will always have an alcoholic component. We all have the same flawed thinking pattern. Some meetings are very powerful when someone shares his or her fears. It's important to share our fears because our brains want us to think that we are different from everyone else in the room. Usually someone will start with a problem or perception and then the rest of the group will relate. Going to a meeting is like looking into a mirror and clearly seeing yourself—you identify with the person speaking because you have experienced the same thing. In doing so you get clarity of thought, even if it is only for that hour. It is powerful and inspiring. What is amazing is that most of us resist the very thing that will help us become whole again. More often than not fear and anger are followed by laughter at the insanity of our lives. If a nonalcoholic were present, he or she might be horrified, but we have to laugh at ourselves, because in doing so we get to see the truth of ourselves. Sharing our thinking helps us to get a clearer view of what is really going on and prepares us for the next twenty-four hours.

ANOTHER ALCOHOLIC DILEMMA

"You cannot resolve a dilemma
with the same mind that created it."
— Albert Einstein

Here is a truism from my friend Clyde, who has often said about his past, "I always wanted to be judged by my intentions, but all those around me judged me by my actions." How many of us intended not to drink, or not to drink too much? How many of us intended to be home at a certain time, only to have broken that promise by hours? How many of us intended to do a lot of things, only to fall short?

Clyde reminded me, "We cannot think our way out of alcoholism; we have to act our way out." It is through action, not words, that we regain the trust and respect of our families and friends. Since sobriety is a daily reprieve, we have to start each day with intentions that are followed by actions. We cannot just intend to go to a meeting; we actually have to get up and go. We cannot intend to call our sponsor; we have to pick up the phone and call. If we do this every day, then before we know it, we have developed a new habit. As Matthew Kelly teaches us, "If you want to change your life, then change your habits."

UNCOMFORTABLE

"Courage is the ability to do the right thing, all the time,
no matter how painful or uncomfortable it might be."
— *Tony Dungy*

One of the things I learned about alcoholics is that we are by nature uncomfortable. No matter where we are or what we are doing, we just don't feel comfortable with life.

Clyde, obviously one of my favorite guys at my seven-a.m. meeting, said, "I've had the same job for twenty-three years and I always think that today is the day that I am going to be fired. I've lived in the same house for eighteen years and I still haven't unpacked one of my suitcases. I have been married for thirty-three years and I am still not certain that she is the one."

Ray O'Keefe, the great AA speaker, said, "When I came out of my mother's birth canal and into the world it was just too loud, and I needed something to quiet it down." That is what I mean by uncomfortable. When I was in my middle teenage years, I had to be hospitalized on three occasions over a period of four years for severe back spasms.

The doctors could not figure it out. I could not stand or walk and was bedridden. I was admitted to the hospital, given muscle relaxants, and had weights placed at each end of the bed to stretch me out until the muscles relaxed.

There was no diagnosis then, but I now know that I suffered from anxiety. I was simply not comfortable in my own skin. As with Ray, life was too loud for me. I could not handle it; my body just reacted to the stress. These were physical manifestations of that discomfort, along with abdominal pain, irritable bowel syndrome, and difficulty sleeping. I never connected the stress and anxiety to alcoholism; however, like many addicts, when I had that first drink, the feeling of relief was so overwhelming that I pursued it for more than twenty-five years, until I was institutionalized.

LONELINESS

"The most terrible poverty is loneliness an
the feeling of being unloved."
— *Mother Teresa*

The global health service company Cigna released the results of a survey it conducted on the impact of loneliness
in the United States. Some of the conclusions:

- 46 percent of Americans report sometimes or always feeling alone. Forty-seven percent report feeling left out.

- 27 percent of Americans rarely or never feel as
  though there are people who really understand
  them.

- 43 percent sometimes or always feel that their relationships are not meaningful and that they are iso-
  lated from others.

- 20 percent report that they rarely or never feel close
  to people or that there are people they can talk to.

- 53 percent of Americans have meaningful in-per-
  son social interaction, such as an extended conver-

sation with a friend or spending quality time with family, on a daily basis.

- Generation Z, adults ages 18 to 22, is the loneliest generation and claims to be in worse health than older generations.

Social media use alone is not a predictor of loneliness; respondents defined as very heavy users of social media have a loneliness score that is not markedly different from the score of those who never use social media.

Bill Wilson and Bob Smith knew all those years ago that alcoholics need to have face-to-face contact with other alcoholics on a daily basis in order to remain sober. With Facebook, Twitter, Instagram, and all the apps on our smartphones and computers, we humans still need more connection. Healthy fellowship breeds healthy thinking. Eye contact helps us to speak more openly and honestly about how we are feeling.

Alcoholics are escapists. For us, the world as it presents itself is just too stressful, and we like to escape from the difficulties of life. Whatever problems or anxieties we face disappear with alcohol and drugs—only to return the next day. The cycle then repeats itself until the battle with this illness is eventually lost or recovery is achieved.

Many alcoholics are by nature isolators. I heard a line at a meeting that resonated with me: Being alone in your own head is like being in a darkroom, and the only thing to do there is to process negatives. By ourselves, we alcoholics tend to dwell on the negative. It takes contact with other recovering people to see the reality of our lives. Being part of a group is beneficial to recovery.

This subject of loneliness is not spoken about a great deal in AA, but it can have a powerful impact on the life of a recovering person. Alcoholics who are out in their communities and spending time in bars have a false sense of connection. For me the setting, the lighting, the glasses, the bar, the whole package gives me a sense of being part of something.

Loneliness is not just a problem for alcoholics; it is a worldwide problem. There are more people on this earth than ever, but many are more alone than ever. In the United States it seems everyone has a phone keeping them connected with everyone else, and yet we are not truly connected. Loneliness is a major problem. Being alone in your room with a phone is not being connected. Being in a room with other people speaking honestly and openly creates true human connection. As humans we all strive to be connected.

Recovering alcoholics recognize early on that most of

their friendships were connected to drinking, and when the drinking ended, so did many of those relationships. Before learning to connect with others in recovery, there can be a period of time when loneliness sets in. People can get lost when they're all alone. Most do not just jump into AA with both feet. If they are anything like me, they may start with one foot in AA and the other still planted in their old world, not certain yet if this were the life they would really like to live.

Most are hesitant to admit having these feelings of loneliness, or to discuss them. It takes courage to do so, and to be willing to let those who are also in recovery connect with them. Bill Wilson and Bob Smith knew this and spent their time connecting with others. Alone in one's head is about the worst place an alcoholic can reside.

Drinking and using drugs gave me a false sense of connection. For normal people, a few drinks melt away inhibition and allow for connection. For alcoholics it is pretty much the only way they connect. Twelve-step meetings represent an opportunity to learn what genuine human connection is about.

My friend likes to say that when he is overwhelmed with the problems of life, he retreats to his couch, where he can sit for hours thinking about his problems and trying to figure a way out. It is not until he gets off the couch and speaks with other recovering people that he gets answers.

POSITIVE AND NEGATIVE ENERGY

"What lies behind us and what lies before us are tiny matters compared to what lies within us."
— *Ralph Waldo Emerson*

Alcoholism is a progressive illness. It may start with the alcoholic being a part of the crowd and very much involved with those around him or her. Over time, all who suffer from this illness eventually find themselves alone. This is an illness of loneliness and isolation. Most who succumb to it die alone.

I have learned over the years that I have a spirit, and at times I was asked when I was in an alcoholic state if I was all right. My initial response was, "Yes, why do you ask?" I was then told that I did not seem to be myself. The energy body was filled with negativity, and most often I was unaware of it.

Like all human beings, I have an energy body. When I am grateful and happy, that energy is radiated to those around me. When the energy turns to negativity, it becomes apparent to all in my presence that I am not all right.

Throughout my journey I have had many episodes of alcoholic thinking, which is distorted thinking that I am not fully aware of at the time. I have not had a drink, but I am certain that if I remained in that state, eventually I would have picked up a drink or a drug. The only thing that has saved me from myself is the fact that I have never stopped going to meetings, which allows those around me to see in me that I cannot see in myself.

I have a friend, Frank, who has been with me on this journey for more than thirty years. Recently he came into a meeting early in the morning, and at the same moment two of us asked him what was wrong. He immediately said, "Nothing." It was apparent from the negative energy coming off him that he was not OK. Later at that same meeting Frank admitted to being in a foul state of mind and that he had to talk about it. I can show that same energy, positive or negative, and those around me can detect it.

Dr. Robert Friedman, a former medical director at Marworth, explained to me that alcoholics and addicts in active addiction turn that negative energy inward so that it becomes self-destructive.

I am safe as long as I am in good spiritual condition. That means I am not self-centered and selfish and that I am more concerned about those around me. That is why we are counseled that when are in an alcoholic state, we must get out of ourselves and help another human being. Bill Wilson and Bob Smith recognized this early on and reached out to the suffering alcoholics around them. Those gestures ensured that they could remain sober by helping others.

The major problem with this illness is that if we are in the right spiritual condition, we only get a twenty-four-hour reprieve, no matter how much time we have. This is not compatible with the idea that we can do this on our own, nor is it compatible with using mind-altering drugs. As I have said, I wholeheartedly agree with the need for medication-assisted treatment until the patient can be stabilized, especially with the seriousness of the opioid crisis. However, the long-term use of these medications will not lead to a healthy sobriety. In order to become fully aware of ourselves, we need a human connection, and we need to have a clear mind, not one that has been altered.

PROGRESSION

"Physicians who are familiar with Alcoholism agree there is no such thing as making a normal drinker out of an alcoholic."
— *Alcoholics Anonymous*

I have been told that with each relapse it becomes more difficult to get back on the path of recovery. The alcoholic thinking becomes more distorted, and surviving the relapse only makes the alcoholic more certain that the next time will be different that somehow, they will be to drink or use successfully without any negative consequences.

I met a woman who was in recovery for thirteen years, and when her life became filled with stressful situations, she stopped paying attention to her recovery. She lived in Maryland but was originally from Pennsylvania. She eventually rationalized that she could start to drink again but only in Pennsylvania. Of course, she did not share these thoughts with anyone. So, for two years she did just that—she drank only when she was in Pennsylvania. It was not long before she found herself making more excuses to travel to Pennsylvania. Eventually she started to drink in Maryland, and it got worse. Finally, she got back into AA, but she told us that this time it was more difficult to remain sober. She would not drink for a day or two and then would drink again. Her mind kept telling her that she could control her drinking, and she would relapse.

The last time I saw her she had been sober for a few weeks, but she explained that the road to recovery was much more difficult. Her story only confirmed for me that this illness is progressive and that without help we simply cannot beat it.

Alcoholism progresses whether we are drinking or not. We have all heard countless stories of men and women who have stopped drinking or using drugs for long periods of time, sometimes twenty or thirty years. When they relapse, it is only a short time before they are drinking or using again as if they had never stopped. The progression is baffling.

COMMUNICATION AND CONNECTION

"Sometimes, reaching out and taking someone's hand
is the beginning of a journey. At other times,
it isallowing another to take yours."
— *Vera Nazarian*, The Perpetual Calendar of Inspiration

When under the influence, most alcoholics feel connected. If they're at a bar, they can speak to almost anyone about anything, with thoughts and opinions that they feel are profound and to the point. They can grab a stranger and talk all night. There are other alcoholics who drink by themselves, communicating only with themselves, reliving their slights and resentments. They are sure that their thoughts are clear and that they know what they are doing. Neither type has the faintest idea what real communication is.

At one point I attended a marriage encounter weekend with Harville Hendrix and Helen Hunt, relationship therapists and life partners who teach couples, alcoholic and nonalcoholic alike, how to communicate. Though reluctant, I agreed to go, and once I was there, my eyes were opened. At the first weekend retreat there were about forty couples, of all ages and backgrounds. A few years later my wife and I attended a second weekend, where there were six couples (three of these couples had a recovering alcoholic).

I was much more comfortable the second weekend, after what I learned at the first encounter. What I learned is that I had to be willing to listen to my partner and then repeat what she said. It was amazing to me that more often than not, I did not accurately interpret what she had said, and the exercise had to be repeated until I clearly heard what she was trying to communicate to me. I must admit that even having been taught those tools, I am very reluctant to utilize them. My brain hijacks healthy thinking and reverts to its old pattern of denial and blame.

At one point in the weekend Harville showed a psychological study of a mother and baby that was done many years ago (it would not be repeated today because it would be unethical). The baby was about twelve months old, sitting in a highchair. The mother's face was at the level of the baby's as she smiled and held the baby's hands. The baby was active and full of happiness. In the next segment the mother was told to stare at the baby with a blank face and to make no move to engage. At first the baby just tried to get her attention with rapid hand movements, then apparent frustration, and finally crying, clamoring for the mother's attention. The mother's expression never changed.

Harville and Helen explained that when we come into the world we are connected to our mothers. At some point along the way that connection is broken, and for the rest of our lives we are attempting to reconnect with those we love. Many are successful in attaining heathy connections, but if you are an alcoholic then that early loss of connection is only compounded and more difficult to re-establish.I learned from that experience that I too was longing to connect, particularly to my wife and children, and that alcohol and drugs gave me a false sense of connection. When I stopped using, I did not know how to connect in any real sense. Recovery was the first step, and as the AA book says, after putting down the drink the real work begins.

In two days of marriage therapy my wife and I were taught to listen to each other, to ask if we understood each other and what was said, to repeat what the other said, and then to have empathy for each other instead of being defensive. I learned a great deal. I have tried to put those tools to use, though I know I fall short. I'm still working on it.

LOVE

"Love is our true destiny. We do not find the meaning of Life by ourselves alone—we find it with another."
— *Thomas Merton*, Love and Living

What is love? In the experiment with the mother and baby, the mother was connected with the baby, and then intentionally she became disconnected. The baby first tried to get her attention, then cried for it and became more and more agitated as the mother remained unavailable to him. The conclusion of that study was that at some point along our journey most of us experience such a disconnect, and we spend the rest of our lives trying to regain that early feeling of connection.

Most alcoholics or addicts will tell you that their first experience with a substance was wonderful even if they wound up vomiting at the end of the night. We spend the rest of our lives trying to recapture that original feeling of connectedness.

Most of us confuse sex with love, although it is a great way to express our deepest feelings to another human, as

long as it is not selfish. My experience has shown me that alcoholics have a difficult time with intimacy, and if we are to be truly intimate with another human being, then we must drop our defenses and be open to that other person in more than just a physical sense.

I love my wife, our children, and all of our very large extended family. That was not so when I was actively addicted. I would often hear men and women in treatment say that they must get out because they missed their spouses and children. This was another self-deception. Most of us were not present in their lives while we were active. We must lie to ourselves before we lie to others. I am certain that I said the same thing in treatment, except the truth was that my family was a liability to me when I was drinking, because they interfered with my self-serving plans to drink. My sponsor, Bud, told me that I was at my best when I practiced "more you and less me." This is not easy for alcoholics because we are by nature self-centered and selfish.

As I mentioned, I never cried much growing up; it was not allowed. I cried the first night I was in rehab, October 20, 1986. I cried in my bed in the middle of the night because I felt desperate and hopeless. I did not know at that time that this was not the end, but a new beginning. I cried again at the passing of my mother and father be-

cause I came to realize how much they had sacrificed for their children, and that they had done the best they could. I cried yet again at the passing of my youngest brother, Andrew, who died of cancer at the age of fifty-one. I realized how deeply I loved him and how much I would miss him. Although it was difficult, I was grateful that I could feel those profound emotions. I must admit, however, that feeling emotion is still foreign to me and requires effort on my part to allow myself to feel.

Let me say a few more words about efforts to recognize emotion. When I was growing up, there were just too many of us, and there really was no time for any of us to express emotion. If I was going to express any emotion, I was told, "Knock it off or I will give you something to cry about." That message only trained me to bury those emotions deep within myself, to the point that I simply did not recognize them. Alcohol helped me to feel but not in a healthy way. Any emotions I felt were distorted and unnatural. Eventually I, like most alcoholics, simply could not feel emotions. Self-centeredness had taken over my thought patterns. To this day I still have difficulty expressing my emotions.

In order to identify what I am feeling, I have to first admit that there is something wrong. That is the first problem, because my mind is sending me all sorts of messages warning me not to talk, telling me it is not important, or if I do talk I will look foolish, or I will show weakness and will be controlled. Of course, none of this is true, but it is my reality at that time.

If, however, I am at a meeting and someone else is willing to express an emotion, I can often identify with that person and actually recognize that very same emotion in myself. What is more interesting to me is that I have come to recognize that I have many deep emotions within me; it just continues to be a struggle to express them.

BEING THERE

"The best time to plant a tree was 20 years ago.
The second-best time is now."
— *Chinese Proverb*

In the 1979 film *Being There*, Peter Sellers played the part of a simpleminded gardener, Chance, who resides in the townhouse of his wealthy supporter. His only education is through television. When his boss dies, Chance is forced to leave. He winds up on the street, and his simple wisdom captivates everyone he encounters. It is a great satire. I do not wish to give too much away, but it's worth watching, for many reasons.

What is so powerful is that Chance can only live in the moment, while all those around him are living in the past and the future. It reinforces how powerful being in the moment can be.

THE GIFT OF AWARENESS

"Awareness is all about restoring your freedom to choose
what you want instead of what your past imposes on you."
— *Deepak Chopra*

It was not easy for me to see the problem. It took time and effort for me to finally get the true gift of recovery: awareness. When I was drinking with my friends the week before being institutionalized, I had no idea that I was an alcoholic. Even though I resisted, I finally capitulated and agreed to go into a treatment center. For the next forty-two days the counselors worked to break through my wall of denial so that I could finally admit that I was an alcoholic and needed help. I was made aware.

That awareness was fragile. Over the next year or two I attended meetings almost every day, and with that my awareness increased and I was able to live life without picking up a drink or a drug. Now, years later, I understand how tenuous this awareness is.

Geisinger Marworth Treatment Center has a professional program for health care workers. Most doctors and other health care workers are treated for up to three months—longer than most because it can be difficult to break their ego and denial. Many get sober and go on to lead productive lives. However, there are many others who do not make it past the three-year mark. Over that three-year period memories fade, but the alcoholic brain never weakens. That old thinking pattern lies dormant, waiting for your guard to drop. We stop sharing our innermost thoughts and our enemy, rationalization, goes back to work, stronger than ever. What I've noticed is that health care professionals think of their journey as a string of exams—pass this course and move on to the next. At that point many stop paying attention to this chronic, progressive, deadly disease. Complacency dooms sobriety. As in the past, the doctor is back in her head and starts to believe that she is smart and what did they know. The ending is never a happy one.

I knew a minister who had almost died as a result of his drinking. After a long hospitalization for damage to his body and then a rehabilitation center for treatment, he became sober. He told us one morning at a meeting that he was celebrating one year of recovery and that he was finally starting to feel like his old self. However, he reported that at the breakfast table that morning he asked his wife if she thought his treatment for alcoholism was an "over-correction." She looked at him in shock and said, "Do you not remember that you almost died in the hospital?" He replied, "Oh, that." Again, the way we think is confounding.

Three things happen in the alcoholic's mind when he stops being connected to others in recovery. First, he starts to minimize what happened. This, of course, is done in his own head; he doesn't talk to anyone. Then he convinces himself that this new way of living is a mistake. Next, he starts to intellectualize: "I'm a doctor, I'm smart. Now that I have all this information and experience, I will approach my use differently." And finally, by himself he will begin to romanticize his drinking or drug use until finally he starts again down the path of self-destruction. If he is being monitored, he will wait until the monitoring ends and then let the head games begin. Unfortunately, many of the patients who come into recovery are forced there by families, courts, or licensing agencies. Many of them simply comply but do not acknowledge their illness. If they continue to comply without committing, there is a very high probability that they will not remain sober for an extended period of time.

Eventually, the health care professional starts to resent what he or she feels are unfair and burdensome rules and requirements. That resentment results in anger directed at others. The person starts to think that she "passed" the sobriety course, and complacency sets in. Compliance eventually leads to more resentment for being forced to do the very things that help her maintain sobriety. Meeting attendance falls off, contact with other alcoholics stops, and the worst thing happens: The alcoholic starts to think that she is not like those other recovering people and that she can manage her own life. Eventually many of these professionals pick up a drug or a drink and wind up with ruined careers and in some cases death. The 12-step program works great—if you work it. It is about total surrender and compliance. Just like the diabetic, if you don't "take your medication" as directed, there are consequences. That awareness, the gift that the alcoholic worked so hard for, has been lost. A relapse is most likely on the horizon.

What I learned is that the gift of awareness is truly that: a gift. It must be nurtured every day. Without effort it fades. Since sobriety is only a twenty-four-hour gift, upon awakening each day the alcoholic has to take action to maintain it. Just thinking about it doesn't work. Meetings, contact with a sponsor, talking to another alcoholic, prayer, and meditation are all positive action steps.

By being around other recovering alcoholics and sharing how we think and feel, we are able to keep our guard up. That awareness cannot be stored or accumulated; it must be restored daily.

PLEASURE VERSUS HAPPINESS

"Happiness is different from pleasure.
Happiness has something to do with struggling
and enduring and accomplishing."
— *George A. Sheehan*

Alcoholics and addicts are wired for pleasure, in an attempt to achieve happiness.

My brain since childhood was programmed for instant gratification. Growing up, I was driven to be successful and was constantly reminded that my hard work would eventually be rewarded. I can remember how badly I wanted to have fun right then and how that set up conflict with my father. So, after I completed my four years of professional training at the University of Pennsylvania School of Dental Medicine, I joined the US Air Force. After three years in the military, I resumed my training back in New York, where I completed the requirements for my certificate in orthodontics. I was ready to enjoy life at its fullest and without restraint. I still worked hard, but I played even harder. That would eventually be a recipe for disaster. At that time, I could not differentiate between pleasure and happiness.

The pursuit of pleasure is interesting in that the anticipation of pleasure is intense and the experience of it is short-lived. Each pleasurable experience would be fun, but when it was over, a feeling of "Is that all there is?" would set in. Then the desire to reexperience that feeling would take hold, and the process would begin again.

A night of drinking would look like a great adventure, and early on it was, but the next morning would be filled with the misery of a hangover. In the same way, an affair might look very tempting, but the next day would be filled with feelings of guilt and shame for having betrayed one's spouse.

Happiness, on the other hand, is a long-term deal. Bill Wilson and his crowd were careful with the words they chose. They promised reasonable happiness, which was the result of doing the next right thing long enough. That is not what the alcoholic wants to hear, but it is what he or she needs to hear. Happiness is not the up-and-down pursuit of pleasure, but a feeling of satisfaction for the time spent working to stay sober. Happiness is an inside job, and I wasted years working on the outside.

When someone asked Father Martin, a Catholic priest

who helped thousands of people trying to recover, how he could regain his self-esteem, he told him to simply continue to do the next right thing long enough and it would just happen. Eventually that happiness leads to contentment.

Recently I read an obituary of a man who won $315 million in a Powerball jackpot. He took a lump sum of $113.4 million after taxes. It wasn't long before he became embroiled in scandal and lawsuits. He was constantly asked for money and eventually was unable to trust anyone. He was often quoted as saying he wished he had ripped up the ticket. Many of us think money is the answer to our problems and will lead to happiness. For this man it ruined his life.

Over two thousand years ago, Aristotle taught that to achieve happiness, we need to find a purpose, and in doing so to realize our potential. According to the philosopher, happiness is not about well-being but instead is a lasting state of contentment, which should be the final goal of the human experience. By changing our behavior patterns, we will eventually become a-better-version-of-ourselves. This lesson remains the same more than two thousand years later.

MORE ON AWARENESS

"Experience is not what happens to you;
it is what you do with what happens to you."
— *Aldous Huxley*

My friend Dick shared at a meeting one morning that when he was young and still drinking, he was called to the principal's office because of his drinking. The biggest problem was that he was not a student; he was the teacher. That experience struck me because it pointed out just how unaware the active alcoholic is of himself. Others can see clearly how out of control our lives are, but we seem totally unaware of it.

I spent the first thirty years of my life growing up and going to school to study for my orthodontic profession. So, when I began my private practice at the age of thirty, my thought was that now that I had finished the difficult road, it was time for me to enjoy the benefits of my labors to the fullest. So, from the age of thirty to forty-two, I tried to raise a family, work, play golf, and drink. I look back and I'm amazed at just how difficult that was to do.

My alcoholism progressed rapidly, and I never gave it a thought. Like most of those on the path of addiction, I had rules: only drink on weekends, never drink the night before seeing patients, never drink early in the day, know when I have had enough. Like all alcoholics, I eventually broke every rule. My point is that during those years I was never truly aware of what was happening. By the time I was forty, those around me were starting to notice that I was not OK. When confronted with any concerns about drinking and its effect on my life, I was defensive or minimized them. My defense was that I was going to work every day and my health appeared to be reasonably OK. I knew better than any of those around me. In short, I had absolutely no awareness of myself. I had become a totally self-centered and selfish alcoholic.

The gift of awareness comes, slowly, with each day of sobriety. The unfortunate problem is that as an alcoholic I cannot hold on to it without help. Since this is a daily reprieve and we only have twenty-four hours, I can wake up the next day with or without awareness. I get an opportunity to identify it and to realize that I am not always in actual reality but only in my own reality. My friend Leo always points out to people in early recovery, "It is not what you know that gets you in trouble, it's what you think you know that is not so." It is one of the most profound problems of alcoholism. I cannot see myself, and my mind is always trying to revert to my natural alcoholic state. I have been forewarned many times along this path. I cannot think myself out of this illness; I must act myself out of it, and to do that, I must be aware of myself. Becoming self-aware is one of the greatest challenges of recovery, because without it the alcoholic starts down the slippery slope of relapse.

HABITS

"You'll never change your life until you change something you do daily. The secret of your success is found in your daily routine."
— *John C. Maxwell*

Upon leaving the rehabilitation center I was told that I had to change my life—not some things, but everything. When I was drinking and using drugs, I smoked, ate poorly, kept terrible hours, had poor sleeping habits, and was generally irritable, restless, and discontented. I would classify these as bad habits. I had to cultivate new habits.

Alcohol is a sugar. When I stopped drinking, like most alcoholics, I still craved sugar. I had started living alone in an apartment, where I had a bed and a small table and chairs, with a pretty good-size kitchen and lots of cabinets. I had been living there for about two months when I opened a couple of cabinet doors and said to myself, "Who is buying all these pies?" That would be me. I said to myself, "This has got to stop." A few months later I opened my freezer and realized that I had accumulated ten half gallons of ice cream. Again, I said to myself, "Who is buying all this ice cream?" Again, that would be me. It took time for me to change my eating habits so that they were not filled with unnecessary sugar. My body was calling out for sugar and I was responding even though I was not fully aware of what I was doing.

I was once at an event with Matthew Kelly, where he was the principal speaker. It was not for alcoholics; it was for people of faith. He said at one point, "If you want to change your life, change your habits." He paused and then repeated that statement three times. I was stunned, for I certainly had developed some pretty bad habits while drinking. I was drawn to Matthew, and over the years he has taught me a great deal, but that first night he gave me the information I needed to implement the changes necessary to survive this illness.

I figured out that when I was drinking, I spent at least twenty to thirty hours a week at that endeavor. I never complained about it; I only wanted more hours. I now had to cultivate new habits, primarily by going to meetings. I decided that I needed to attend three to five meetings a week. That is three to five hours compared to twenty to thirty hours of drinking, yet there are still days when I think that's way too many meetings.

I had to develop new sleep habits. I was told that I needed to go to bed at the same time every night and to get eight hours of sleep. In my drinking days, I slept anywhere between two and ten hours, depending on the damage and the time available.

I ate poorly when active, so I also had to change my eating habits. I now needed to eat healthier foods and on a normal schedule. It was not easy. I loved my bad habits and I embraced them.

It took time, patience, and help from those around me to change, slowly but surely. My life did change, and I now cherish those good habits. I look back and I am horrified that I was on such an awful path of self-destruction. Concerning meetings, I learned that they had to be a habit, that I could not just decide whether I should go or not. If that were the case, I would not go. So, I now have a schedule of the same meetings every week. I don't have to think about whether I should go or not; I just go. If it's Monday I am at the seven-a.m. meeting; I don't even have to think about it. These new habits have served me well.

Like most, I found it very intimidating to share early in recovery. I would sit there knowing that I should speak, but I just could not find the courage to expose my innermost feelings. It took time, but eventually it became easier. What is most interesting to me is that even today, when I wake up in that alcoholic state and I am sitting in a meeting, the internal dialogue with myself will go like this: "First, why did you bother going to a meeting? What are you here for? You have nothing to say. These people are idiots. You do not belong here; you are not like them."

This goes on until I say four very important words: "I am not OK."

That is when the healing starts.

INTIMACY

"There's nothing more intimate in life than simply being understood. And understanding someone else."
— *Brad Meltzer*, The Inner Circle

You would think alcoholics would want to be connected to those closest to them. Wrong—alcoholics fear intimacy. Just recently I realized after all this time that I have a fear of rejection; it probably comes from my childhood. As I've mentioned, as the firstborn I felt a great deal of pressure to succeed. My mother loved me unconditionally and never abandoned me, no matter what the situation. My father, with his fear that I might fail, drove me, and I feared his rejection if I did not meet his expectations of me. I believe his motive was good, but I don't think he realized how profoundly that would affect the rest of my life.

In my early years, if I was dating someone and I sensed that she was going to dump me, I made sure to end the relationship before she had the chance. Looking back, I realize that I simply could not handle being abandoned.

In my marriage if I sense that my wife is unhappy with my behavior, my first thought is that we need to get a divorce. I would rather flee than face what I think would be too difficult to talk about. It is amazing to me that those childhood experiences can still color my judgment and keep me locked up in my mind. When I am in that state it seems impossible to talk. When I finally come out of the prison of my mind, I sometimes have an overwhelming flood of emotion that seems to be coming out of nowhere.

When actively using drugs or alcohol, one can completely connect to total strangers, although it is not a real connection. Under the influence we can get into deep discussions about everything, even the meaning of life. Take drugs and alcohol out of the mix and there may be no conversation at all. When sex is involved, all inhibitions are abandoned, and self-gratification is paramount. So, the alcoholic thinks she is capable of intimacy. Wrong. This is far from the truth. Having a deep personal, intimate relationship is a challenge. As a result, when the alcoholic starts to recover, she is typically filled with uncertainty, is extremely uncomfortable, and has difficulty with truly intimate relationships, particularly with a spouse or children. Is it that much harder to be intimate in reality than in an altered state? Feelings are extremely difficult to experience and process. Doing something for another without the expectation of payback is foreign.

Because alcoholics tend to be controlling, particularly when they are active or in an alcoholic state, it can be difficult for those around them, especially family members, to deal with them. One of the common character defects is super sensitivity and difficulty accepting criticism, constructive or not. It is a combination of control, fear, and reluctance to engage. My wife of thirty years was the first person to call out my pattern of avoiding intimacy. She said that I do four things to avoid an intimate conversation, or when she is trying to help me change my behavior pattern:

1. I subdue her with a response that has anger in it.
2. I blame others or circumstances that I believe are beyond my control, or I make excuses.
3. I make my pronouncement as though it is fact and then walk away from the conversation, and if I am angry enough, I retreat into my interior cave and try to figure out how I am right, and she is wrong.
4. I stay in the cave until I calm down; it could be an hour, a week, or a month. Then I exit the cave and act like nothing happened. Meanwhile she has been

outside waiting for me, hoping to talk. She knows how to communicate; I don't. Over time those retreats into the cave have become shorter, because experience has taught me that it solves nothing. It is just my fear of intimacy and sensitivity to any criticism that drives me there.

Because I am at times blocked from recognizing my emotions by an irrational fear of losing control, I have been advised to utilize the "three C's" when I find myself becoming resistant and shutting down:

1. Consider
2. Compromise
3. Change

The problem is that as a self-centered alcoholic I do not want to consider someone else's thoughts or ideas. The idea of talking about the problem does not enter my mind. So, the first thing I must do is to open mind to whatever is being presented. Because of this self-centered fear, I also am resistant to compromise. It has to be my way or no way at all. There is usually more than one way to approach a problem and I must be open to other avenues. And as all alcoholics know, we are resistant to change, which goes all the way back to that original intent to protect our alcoholism. It can be very frustrating to those we love when this state of mind is active. The problem is that this is part of being alcoholic, and from what I have experienced with other recovering people, this behavior never completely leaves us.

The only hope is that with some awareness we can break through this resistance and begin to create healthy relationships. Change is possible and it goes back to the first question that is asked when one enters treatment, "What are you willing to do".

The answer should be," Whatever it takes."

My responses now all depend on my spiritual condition. When I am healthy, I respond appropriately; when I am in an alcoholic state, there is some risk of fleeing to the cave. Matthew Kelly wrote a book called *The Seven Levels of Intimacy*, a great resource for determining one's level on the intimacy scale. Seven is ideal; most of us, including me, are at level one or two. It takes work, sacrifice, and openness to begin to learn how to be intimate emotionally with another person. I've finally learned to say, "I love you." It took a combination of therapy, working the 12 steps, and being uncomfortable in my own skin to finally start to share my feelings. Doing so has been difficult because I was brought up to stuff those feelings and just carry on. Most of the time I could not even identify exactly what I was feeling. That blocking behavior I was taught early on in my life made it difficult to experience true intimacy. Today, having realized that resistance is futile, I have reluctantly reached out for professional help.

BALANCE

"Life is a balanced system of learning and evolution. Whether pleasure or pain; every situation in your life serves a purpose. It is up to us to recognize what that purpose could be."
— *Steve Maraboli*

I often hear people in recovery say they are trying to get more balance in their lives. There was a very wise counselor at Marworth, Theo, who was sober for many years. I happened to be at a meeting with her when someone in the group brought up the topic of balance. I will never forget what Theo said: There is no such thing as balance, only the constant attempt to gain it. She explained that life is like walking on a balance beam—you try to walk as steadily on the beam as you can, only to fall to one side or the other. You then climb back on and start again. This is life. We are all walking on the balance beam, and the attempt to achieve a balanced life is a worthy endeavor. Again, the aim is progress, not perfection.

DEPRESSION AND GRATITUDE

"The struggle ends when gratitude begins."
— *Neale Donald Walsch*

I once called my sponsor to report that for no apparent reason, I felt terribly down. I rattled off what I thought were my symptoms: tiredness, irritability, an uneasy feeling about life, sadness, and a feeling of doom. He listened closely, and as soon as I finished, he said, "I know what is wrong with you. You have melancholy." I was shocked and asked what he meant. He said it is common for alcoholics to suffer through periods of melancholy or depression as they travel the path of recovery. Recovery is not a consistent, uphill trajectory; it's more like the stock market, a bumpy, up-and-down journey that over time steadily gets better.

It has always amazed me that when I get into these periods, if I do not reach out to my sponsor, I tend to remain in the funk. When I talk about it and shine the light of day on it, I start to work my way back out of the cave. I have to remember that I am basically an escapist, and when I do not feel OK, I want to change that, which can lead to all sorts of substances or behaviors that will hurt me.

The most potent antidote to melancholy is gratitude. When I can see the reality of my life, then I can survive those dark periods. Without help, however, I am not sure that I could recognize melancholy for what it is: simply a feeling that I can work my way out of.

There are those for whom the feeling is more serious than melancholy and who need treatment or some type of antidepressant medication. It is important that the recovering person seek help from a psychiatrist or psychologist who is well versed in treating recovering alcoholics and addicts. Unfortunately, there are still many health care professionals who do not understand the disease of alcoholism and the proper ways to diagnose and treat it. As such, if the recovering person needs to be on antidepressants, he or she must be monitored closely so as not to create another addiction.

THE-BEST-VERSION-OF-MYSELF

"Anything or anyone that does not help you to become
the-best-version-of-yourself is too small for you."
— Matthew Kelly

Matthew Kelly has spoken to hundreds of thousands of people around the world, some of whom are alcoholics, most of whom are not. One of his most persistent themes is the very important goal of becoming "the-best-version-of-yourself."

I was struck by how much his message of becoming the-best-version-of-yourself matters to the recovering person. Certainly, we are not a very good version of ourselves as active alcoholics and addicts. When our self-centered nature runs riot, we ignore the needs of those around us and attend to what we think are our needs. This invariably leads to conflict and chaos.

I realized that this is what I was attempting to do in my recovery. All day, every day, we continue to come to forks in the road. Going one way would make us better versions of ourselves; going the other would make us lesser versions of ourselves.

Think about this. As alcoholics we tend to make choices all the time that make us worse versions of ourselves. Many of these poor decisions lead down a path that ends in the hospital, jail, or even death.

Becoming the-best-version-of-ourselves is a radical change for an alcoholic; hence the need for a sponsor or another recovering person. The fact that the alcoholic cannot see himself makes it difficult for him to make the right choice. Opening up to another person and being willing to follow direction gives him a better chance to make the right choice. If he does this long enough, these everyday decisions will become easier.

CELEBRATING RECOVERY

"People spend a lifetime searching for happiness: looking for
peace. They chase idle dreams, addictions, religions, even
other people, hoping to fill the emptiness that plagues them.
The irony is the place they ever needed is within."
— *Romona Anderson*

Most AA groups periodically recognize their members for their time in sobriety, from months in the beginning to years as they go through their entire journey. Like most, I have celebrated at different times both to be aware of my own progress and to encourage those just starting out.

I usually had my sponsor give me my chip, but at my twentieth anniversary I asked my wife to give it to me. I thought it would be nice for her to have the opportunity to get up and say a few words about me. My assumption was that without any prompting, she would tell everyone what a great job I had done and how much she admired me.

We came to the front of the room and with chip in hand she looked at the crowd and then at me and said, "Wow!

This early sobriety is a bitch." As the audience laughed, I smiled, although on the inside I was shocked. She went on to say some very heartfelt things about me, but it was another example of me not being able to see the reality of my own life. We alcoholics can be difficult to live with on a daily basis. Her speech and delivery got a good laugh, and later when I thought about it, I realized how accurate it was. This was a challenging path, but it was worth it. Later on, I heard someone say that his wife told him, "You've come such a short distance in such a long time." Ouch.

THOUGHT PATTERNS

*"When you arise in the morning think of what a privilege it
is to be alive, to think, to enjoy, to love ..."*
— *Marcus Aurelius*

Having spent many Tuesday nights at a rehab facility attempting to help recovering health care professionals' weather the difficult time in the center, I have noticed a pattern. There are fears that are the same for all patients. A few of the most common fears are what is going to happen when they leave treatment; whether their spouse will want them back; whether their marriage will survive; how their children will respond; and one of the biggest, what people will think of them.

Spouses have just as many fears and concerns. A very sick individual enters rehab, and the spouse has no idea who's coming back. Will she be different? Will she reject her spouse and leave? Will she remain sober? Will their marriage survive?

Most advice given is simple: Go home, go to a meeting

every day, call your sponsor, and ask your spouse daily what you can do to help. Most important, do not make any major life changes, if possible, for one year. Some relationships survive and some fail, but it is important not to rush to judgment. While we are in rehab our families are left alone and trying to clean up the mess we left in our path. We have to understand that they're probably stressed out. They may think we are taking it easy in rehab, relaxing and getting cared for while they are trying to hold the family together and basically being a single parent. It is a very delicate time. As the alcoholic or addict, we think it is all about us and tend to forget the sacrifices our families make. So, we are counseled to take it easy, to be helpful, to stay connected to other alcoholics. With time and patience, things will start to get better.

Many families need outside help. A therapist can be a great resource to help family members learn how to communicate. Many rehabilitation centers have family programs focusing on how to live with the recovering person. It is important for families to take advantage of these programs. There is no magic formula for how to get better, and recovery does not happen quickly; it happens over time. The damage we inflict on our families happened over time, and repairing that damage takes time, love, and understanding. Families may require Al-Anon or family therapy. Again, healing takes human connection. As alcoholics we have done greater damage to our families than to anyone else around us, and we must be patient and willing to listen to directions in order to heal.

As for returning to work, most of our fears are overblown. The reality is that most of our coworkers already knew we were not all right. Most people around us are very forgiving. When we return from treatment many are relieved to see they got someone back who can now do their job properly. If there is a lack of understanding about this disease and the alcoholic or addict is not welcome back, then it is not a place for the recovering person. It is important to have support from those around us early in recovery.

There was an anesthesiologist who was sent to Marworth for treatment for his alcoholism. He also happened to be the founder of a group of anesthesiologists at the hospital where he practiced. Over time the group had grown to fourteen doctors, and as the founding physician, he was elected president. While he was at the rehabilitation center, the group got together and voted him out. Naturally he was crushed. We counseled him that if the group did not want him back, then that was not where he belonged. We assured him that better times were ahead. It is now six years later, and he is the head anesthesiologist of another group at another hospital.

One of my favorite stories is about a young physician I met at our health care professionals meeting, which is called Caduceus. This meeting allows health care professionals to freely discuss their addiction problems. The caduceus is an ancient Greek or Roman staff, typically with two serpents twined around it, carried by the messenger god Hermes or Mercury. We see it in medical symbols all over the world. These are not official AA meetings, but they can be very helpful to health care professionals early in their recovery.

One of our members was a Vietnamese American named Tom. You may remember the iconic photo of a helicopter on the roof of an apartment building in Vietnam where members of the CIA were staying on the last day of American involvement in the Vietnam War. The building and its staff, along with many loyal Vietnamese, was being evacuated. At that time Tom was six years old. His father was a lieutenant colonel in the Vietnamese army, with a wife and six children. That morning an attaché from the US government went to Tom's house and told his father that he had to leave immediately, or the Vietcong would execute him. He was allowed to take one person with him. He chose his six-year-old son, Tom. Tom was one of the fortunate ones to be rescued on that last day of the United States' withdrawal from Vietnam.

Fast-forward twenty-five years. Tom is a urologist practicing with a group in the Midwest. As a junior member of a large group of urologists, he's working more hours than anyone; he's exhausted and cannot sleep. He asks for help from one of his colleagues, who writes him a script for sleeping pills and continues to write them. Within three months Tom is addicted. He then begins to write his own scripts, which is a felony. One night as he is leaving a pharmacy with his supply of sleeping pills, he is confronted by a group of DEA agents with guns drawn. He is arrested and put in handcuffs. Before he is to be sent to jail, he's allowed to go to a rehab. He chooses Marworth Treatment Center and spends three months there. He is charged with a felony for writing his own scripts, as opposed to a misdemeanor, and his license is revoked (he was not given very good legal advice). After leaving Marworth, he moves to Harrisburg, Pennsylvania, where he sells men's cologne at a department store for two years. He enrolls in the Physicians' Health Program to show his intent to remain sober. With little money and enormous debt, he continues to work hard to stay sober.

Eventually Tom did get a good lawyer, and after incurring more debt, he was able to get his license back. Because of his experience, he left urology and trained in addiction medicine. Today he is recognized as one of the top addiction specialists in the Midwest.

I am aware of countless stories like these, of people who hit rock bottom but end up with lives beyond their wildest dreams. I am also aware of just as many sad endings of people who did not pay attention to this powerful and devastating illness.

HELPING OTHERS

"The meaning of life is to find your gift.
The purpose of life is to give it away."
— *Pablo Picasso*

One of the most glaring defects of character of the alcoholic is his or her self-centeredness. Most often when in active addiction we cannot see it, and if confronted with it, we immediately become the victim. When our spouses or children point out our selfishness, our first thought is, "After all I've done for you," further shielding us from reality.

When we get into recovery, we are instructed to get out of ourselves and look for opportunities to help others, particularly our families and other alcoholics. Very often the first thought there is, "What can I do for you, as long as it does not inconvenience me?" But we must get over our self-centered nature, or it will ruin our lives. It is only when we truly reach out to help someone—without expectations—that we can begin to have some sense of happiness, and in doing so start to become a-better-version-of-ourselves.

SPIRITUALITY

"Science is not only compatible with Spirituality;
it is a profound source of Spirituality."
— *Carl Sagan*, The Demon-Haunted World:
Science as a Candle in the Dark

We are told that if we work the 12 steps of the AA program, we will eventually have a spiritual awakening. Having experienced that awakening, we are then to go forward and help another alcoholic. That awakening could be very profound and moving, or it could be like my own experience, more educational. By that I mean I could not see or understand what was meant by "spirituality." Spirituality is defined in general as a sense of connection to something bigger than us, and it typically involves a search for meaning in life. The problem is that for most active alcoholics, there is no spiritual connection, and the idea that it is required seems impossible to the newcomer in recovery. So early on, my sponsor did not address the spiritual nature; he worked with my thinking and tried to help me get some clarity of thought, which then opened me up to expanding my mind to a higher level of thought. I was able to see that I was not on this journey alone, and things started to happen that seemed connected to something outside me.

The story of something that happened to a friend of mine in recovery has always stayed with me. He had been sober for some time and went to the hospital one morning to perform surgery on an elderly woman. He was concerned that she might be quite anxious, so he decided to go in early to visit her and try to calm her anxiety. As he walked down the hall, he could hear laughter coming from her room.

When he entered her room, he saw a number of nurses around her bed, quite entertained by this very sick woman. After they left, my physician friend sat on the edge of the patient's bed and remarked that he was amazed that she was not nervous. She said to him, "When I was a young nurse working in a hospital in New York I met a man who worked with hopeless alcoholics. I never met anyone like him before or since. He had a way about him that I will never forget, and he had a peace about him that seemed to help those who were deemed to be hopeless." She said she realized then that he was "a messenger from God," and he gave her that sense of peace and trust in a higher power. From that early experience, her life changed, and she trusted that a higher power would take care of her. She said the man's name was Bill Wilson, the founder of AA.

The doctor did something that he never did. He broke his anonymity and said to her, "I am a friend of Bill Wilson's," and she said, "I know. I could tell there was something different about you because of the way you spoke to me and the way you treated me. I knew that there was something different about you and I knew that I could trust you with my life." After the surgery, my friend called me from the hospital to share what had happened. He said the hair on his arms and neck stood right up, and when he told me the story, I had the same experience. What happened to this woman early in her life led her to become aware of a spiritual force that is recognizable in others.

My own spiritual training began in my family, where I was the eldest of twelve children. I grew up in a stable family environment. We went to church every Sunday and every day during the Lenten season. We said the Rosary every night as a family. I have a brother, Joe, who is a Catholic priest and one of the most spiritual people I've ever known. I often wondered where I'd come from because I did not seem to have any spirituality. I was filled with doubt and unable to make a spiritual connection. I was not aware at the time that I was just another budding alcoholic and that, like most, I had little connection to anything. When I was released from treatment, I was told to go to ninety meetings in ninety days and to work the 12 steps, particularly the fourth and fifth. These two steps are done when the alcoholic reviews his life and all his faults, secrets, and defects of character. He then shares all of that with another human being.

Once I did a thorough evaluation of my life and sat down with another recovering alcoholic to share those experiences, I would be able to move forward and complete the remaining steps. I went to meetings, but like many other alcoholics, I put off completing the fourth and fifth steps, for almost two years.

I knew there was a power, some kind of force, but I could not say it was God or any other religious figure. However, I did know that there was something to my awakening, so I decided to try to follow simple laws of nature, like eating right, balancing work and play, exercising, and following some direction for a change. I started to feel better. I was later told that GOD stands for Good Orderly Direction.

I always had a deep fascination with nature and the universe. Over my lifetime we have gone from seeing just our solar system to exploring an ever-expanding universe. This fascinates and overwhelms me. As vast as it is, it is interconnected and gives me a great sense of spirituality. Recently one of my friends, Tony K., said something about his belief in God that I will always remember: "Just think about people in AA meetings as God with skin." I could hold on to that, because I do believe that whatever higher power is present, it speaks to us through other people. If I am willing to listen to those around me who are on the same path as I am, then I will be given good orderly direction—GOD—which has been my experience over the past thirty years.

My spiritual experience has been one of the educational varieties, as it is described in the AA book. Scores of things have happened along the way that I could not explain but that seemed to help me become a-better-version-of-myself. The longer I remained sober, the more I felt a connection to something bigger than I am. I realized

I was part of something that was carrying me along this path in life, and although I could not explain it, that force was in my life. I could no longer deny it. I am not the person I was when I came out of Marworth Treatment Center in 1986. I am more than that. I am becoming a better-version-of-myself. This is a process and a lifelong pursuit.

Early on, I simply could not grasp one of the most spiritual aspects of recovery: living in the moment. Like most, I was either regretting the past or fearing the future. I could not stay where my two feet were planted. It took years for me to learn to be in the present. One day when I was working, I stopped what I was doing and realized that I was totally present in that moment. It was a new experience for me, and I was overcome with gratitude. It can still be a challenge for me to live in the moment but knowing I can do so brings me peace.

I try to remain open to that spiritual voice I hear within me. I still have many unanswered questions, but someone or something has guided me this far, and for that I am grateful.

GRATITUDE

"Gratitude makes sense of our past, brings peace for today, and creates vision for tomorrow."
— *Melody Beattie*

One of the greatest gifts of sobriety is gratitude. Early on, feeling grateful for not being able to drink is almost impossible. In my case the more prominent thought was that my life had been changed forever and I was a victim. How could I possibly be grateful for being deprived of all that I considered worth living for? Harry B., someone who has been around AA for as long as I have, always says that he is grateful because he wakes up every morning without guilt, shame, or fear.

The difficulty is that it takes time for the mind to clear so that we can grasp some sense of awareness. Alcoholic thinking will always be with the alcoholic, but if we continue on the path of recovery, there will come a time when an overwhelming feeling of gratitude comes seemingly out of nowhere. It is elusive but something everyone in recovery can attain if they can continue to be honest with themselves about the reality of their lives.

Many of us have been directed to write a gratitude list and to keep it with us at all times to remind us of everything we should be thankful for, because when things are not going well, we tend to forget how fortunate we truly are. My own experience has taught me that I am more grateful now than I've been at any time along this path.

PRAYER AND MEDITATION

"Prayer is more than meditation. In meditation,
he source is oneself. When one prays, he goes to a source
of strength greater than his own."
— *Madame de Staël*

I would like to say that I am very dedicated to prayer and meditation, but unfortunately, I am not. It is something that I have struggled with throughout my recovery. As my alcoholism grew, my prayer life diminished until there was none. Since I had no idea of who God was, I had no idea to whom I should pray. I had been brought up as a Roman Catholic, but that connection was lost.

After a few years in recovery, I spoke with my brother Joe, the Catholic priest, about my dilemma. First, he told me that he thought AA was one of the greatest spiritual movements of the twentieth century. Second, as far as prayer was concerned, he suggested I simply say thank you to whomever and whatever I believed in, as long as that power was greater than myself. So that is where I started.

Over the years I have been able to pray with gratitude to the God of my understanding. I am now an early riser and am out the door before dawn, usually on my way to a meeting. Where I live, I am most often connected to nature and the beauty of our world. There are some days when I am overwhelmed with gratitude for the opportunity to experience life without impairment.

As far as meditation, it has been just as great a struggle as prayer. Trying to quiet my mind has always been a challenge. It seemed that I always had a free-flowing cascade of thoughts that I had little control of, even with my best efforts to stop them. When I was younger, I could find some moments of being present when I was deep in nature. If I was alone on a lake, alongside a stream, or walking through the woods, I could feel at peace and be somewhat in the moment.

The most profound experience happened the day before I gave up and entered Marworth Treatment Center. I had been considering running away from my problem and entertained the thought of fleeing to Mexico. That Sunday afternoon in mid-October, I drove to a state park and walked deep into the autumn forest. It was a mild, sunny day with a slight breeze. The multicolored leaves from the maples and the oaks were falling rapidly, almost like rain. I stood in the middle of that beautiful forest for what seemed like a very long time, and a feeling of peace came over me like I had never experienced. I knew what I had to do, and I accepted it. That moment will stay with me forever.

My understanding of that power greater than myself is within me because I truly believe I would not have been able to get this far on my own. If I have had a spiritual experience that is of the educational variety (obtaining knowledge over time), then that is enough for me to accept that there is some force that has carried me along.

I continue to strive for prayer and meditation. I started with ten minutes in Matthew Kelly's classroom of silence and have built on it. With the noise of all the distractions in our world, it is difficult to hear the voice inside each of us. By sitting quietly, we allow that inner voice to be heard. For me it has been difficult to quiet all the distractions, but with practice I have seen some improvement. I can now sit in silence and hear the inner voice that was muffled all those years.

You may have noticed that I have mentioned Matthew Kelly a number of times in this book. I believe that he was put into my path early in my recovery. He has been a great source of strength for me, and I consider him to be my spiritual guide. I will forever be grateful for his love and understanding.

RELAPSE

"Failure is the opportunity to begin again more intelligently."
— *Henry Ford*

In an August 2018 *New York Times* opinion piece titled "Addiction Doesn't Always Last a Lifetime," the writer describes a number of people who were addicted and eventually wound up being able to moderately use drugs and alcohol.[16] I respectfully disagree with the premise of the article.

Unfortunately for the alcoholic, the specter of relapse is always there. If you are truly alcoholic, then you simply cannot drink. This is a progressive disease; it never lessens, and it never stops progressing. However, as I mentioned, if you are an abuser of drugs or alcohol there are programs to help manage your use.

One thing that Matthew Kelly taught me early on is that I cannot win the "dialogue with temptation." He was speaking about this to everyone, not just alcoholics, but for us this is of great importance. When an alcoholic or addict thinks about picking up again, he must immediately get that thought out of his head. The longer he debates with himself, the more the barriers drop, and eventually he will succumb to the temptation. If you ask any alcoholic when the relapse began, he will tell you it was long before he actually picked up the drink or drug.

I have listened to countless stories of relapse. In most cases it starts as "controlled" drinking, but invariably, within a short period of time, the alcoholic is drinking like she never stopped. By our own devices, we cannot survive. We need help. That help is readily available every day in AA. We just have to be willing to connect with it. If you are truly alcoholic, it does last a lifetime.

LIFE AFTER ADDICTION

"Don't let the past steal your present."
— *Terri Guillemets*

Like most alcoholics, I was certain that my life had been ruined by my intervention. The thought that I would never be able to drink again was just too overwhelming for me to even begin to grasp. For the month and a half that I was in rehab, I had plenty of time to think and project out about the future. I pondered future events without alcohol and all I could see was myself sullen, deprived, and unable to enjoy myself.

For the first year, I stayed sober out of fear, I think. I was afraid that if I drank again, I would have to go back into rehab. The counselors told me that if I drank, they were going to send me to Alina Lodge, a rehabilitation center in New Jersey that was known for long-term treatment, sometimes up to a year. I kept track of every meeting I went to, first the ninety meetings in ninety days, then five meetings every week. At the end of the first year, I was proud of the milestone, but I was also depressed because

I thought, "Is this all there is?" I remember my sponsor saying that when he first became sober, he was convinced that his life was going to be gray, no more bright lights and fast action. How wrong we both were. We could not see what the future had in store for us. Fortunately, I had other recovering people around me who helped me through those difficult early days.

As I've mentioned, for the first two years I was angry, or so I thought. I was actually afraid, but I was unable to recognize my feelings. Many of us have heard that it can take five years to get your brain back. That is probably pretty accurate. Over those first five years I had to learn how to feel again by gaining some semblance of self-awareness, and how to use better judgment, most often by trusting the advice of others.

Again, there were people around me who gently guided me through the minefield of life. My marriage had failed because of me, and I had to deal with the consequences of my past behavior. My new circle of friends guided me through that. Because of all the damage I had caused in my first marriage, I did not think I would ever marry again. As with most things in my life, what I thought would happen did not happen. I met and fell in love with the most amazing woman, who not only enhanced my life but also helped to raise my children. She was not an alcoholic, and she was naturally kind and caring and willing to work on making our family the best version of itself. We have been together for thirty years. I believe that she too was put in my path.

From year five of sobriety to year ten the fog started to lift, and I began to have feelings of great hope for the future and to experience gratitude. From year ten on, I have made a commitment to keep my habit of five meetings a week and to be open to helping others who are struggling like I was when starting on the path of recovery.

Early in my recovery, someone told me that I should write down what my life would be like in five, ten, and fifteen years. Little did I know just how far off I would be. Now after thirty-four years I can look back in amazement at how wonderful my life has been. There have been deaths and disappointments, but there have been many more positives. My four children survived my alcoholism and are living healthy lives. I have loving relationships with all of them. My orthodontic practice flourished, and I have been blessed with two great professional partners.

THE EFFECTS ON MY FAMILY

"Addiction is a family disease, one person may use,
but the whole family suffers."
— Identity Project.org, 12StepPlanet.com

Remember that I left for rehab on my son's tenth birthday. It is still hard for me to think about that day. I was so self-centered and unaware of the damage I had caused my wife and children. Before my first marriage I had been in a violent auto accident in California and was hospitalized for a month with significant facial damage. The recovery period lasted for six months, and during that time I met someone who was kind and caring to me even with my disfigurement. Looking back, I probably was not ready to be in a relationship, but I went forward and got married. Fortunately, over the course of our fourteen-year marriage four healthy children were born; they have been the greatest gifts of my life. Eventually the relationship broke down because of the progression of my alcoholism. By the end I could only see what I thought were her shortcomings and never was willing to look at my own. It was easier for me to blame my wife for the failure of the marriage. Nothing could be further from the truth. The collapse of that marriage was my fault, although at the time I could not admit it. Marriage counseling failed. I held on to my distorted thinking. It took me many years before I eventually sat down with my ex-wife and apologized for all I had done to destroy that relationship.

After treatment, I moved out and was living alone, with the typical see your children every other weekend scenario. Even though I was no longer drinking, I was not healthy, and it was a very stressful time for all of us. Our children were affected by my alcoholism, as is every family that has a parent with this illness. My son, Matthew, inherited my genes and went down a similar path; he has given me permission to talk about his experience. Our daughters were spared from having the disease of alcoholism. Of course, there were other issues that we have worked through, and they are now healthy adults raising their own children. For their privacy I do not wish to revisit those times. I do believe that without my becoming sober we were all destined to become casualties of this illness. We did ultimately pursue the necessary therapy to address the issues my illness had caused. Over a number of years, some of which were difficult, we confronted our family issues. Today we can actually talk to each other without fear of judgment. It is such a beautiful thing to be able to communicate safely and lovingly.

Our three wonderful daughters turned out to be amazing women and have made every effort to raise healthy families.

Our son's ride was a little rockier. Matthew went from being a solid student to struggling at school and acting out. He eventually wound up at the University of Pittsburgh, but his time there was short-lived.

Like his father, Matthew developed an alcohol and drug addiction. The truth is that his addiction didn't just appear during that freshman year; it had manifested many years earlier. He spent most of his high school years under "house arrest," or grounded, which meant he was unable to truly let loose and live the life of an addict. Once he was "free," it was just a matter of time before he self-destructed. He was barely passing in school and was angry and blaming others for his situation. As a recovering alcoholic, I knew what to do, but as a parent I was frozen in fear. So, I reached out for help. I called Dr. Colangelo, who'd been the director of Marworth during my time there and explained the situation. He told me that I was enabling Matthew's behavior. He said my son was going to die at his present pace and that I had to give him a choice: Get treatment or get out. Matthew refused help, and for the next year his world got smaller and smaller in Pittsburgh, until one night he ended up getting fired from his job at a bar, breaking his hand, and getting kicked out of his apartment because his roommate said he was just too difficult to live with. He had nowhere to go. He had hit his rock bottom.

He eventually called me, and like most alcoholics, he tried to negotiate—*I'll do this, but I won't do that.* Nick had cautioned me not to accept any answer from Matthew except that he would do as he was directed. After a few days of debate, Matthew called and said that he was willing to ask for help. He told me to come and get him; I told him to take a bus home. He went to Clearbrook, a treatment center where Dr. Colangelo was then the director. Matthew was there for fourteen days, and then the decision was made to send him to a more intense and longer-term facility, Blue Mountain House of Hope, in the remote Appalachian Mountains, where he stayed for another four months. This treatment center focused on working the land by digging ditches and building walls. Matthew reported to me that they moved a lot of rocks around. This was a place where serious discipline was valued; it was not a pleasant, spa-like rehab where gentle words of encouragement were shared. At one point I called Nick and protested that Matthew had had enough treatment, and he told me to mind my own business. "Matthew is sick, and he needs help," he said.

After House of Hope, Nick sent Matthew to a halfway house, where he stayed for another two months. That all happened in 1997. Matthew is now twenty-three years sober. He went into treatment four months shy of his twenty-first birthday.

He returned to university and amazingly became an A student. He went on to get an MBA in management and spent a decade of business building and working in international development. He then moved to New York City and received his master's degree in mental health counseling from Fordham University, where he finished at the top of his class. He is now a successful therapist in Washington, D.C., putting all his past experiences to good use. Needless to say, we are enormously proud of him for all he has accomplished since becoming sober.

I could never have imagined that we would have as

strong a relationship as we have today. I think it is because we have both gone through the 12 steps. We have a common language that allows us to communicate so that we hear and respect each other, and compassion is our North Star. In this present moment, we are sober and not fighting anything; we simply are trying to be the-best-versions-of-ourselves. My son has given me great guidance and advised and encouraged me to write this book.

It is not just the way we think that matters. Deepak Chopra says, "The way you think, the way you behave, and the way you eat can influence your life by 30 to 40 years." By the time the addict hits rock bottom, he or she is usually a physical, mental, and spiritual mess. It takes time for all this damage to occur, and it will take time for the body, mind, and spirit to heal. Recovery is not simply the act of stopping the drinking or drugging. It is a process of accepting life on life's terms.

THE GUY IN THE GLASS

"I guess the worst day I have had was when I had to stand
up in rehab in front of my wife and daughter and say,
'Hi, my name is Sam, and I am an addict."
Samuel J. Jackson

When you get what you want in your struggle for self
And the world makes you King for a day,
Then go to the mirror and look at yourself,
And see what that guy has to say.
For it isn't your Father, or Mother, or Wife,
Who judgment upon you must pass.
The feller whose verdict counts most in your life
Is the guy staring back from the glass.
He's the feller to please, never mind all the rest,
For he's with you clear up to the end,
And you've passed your most dangerous, difficult test
If the guy in the glass is your friend.
You may be like Jack Horner and "chisel" a plum
And think you're a wonderful guy,

But the man in the glass says you're only a bum

If you can't look him straight in the eye.

You can fool the whole world down the pathway of years,

And get pats on the back as you pass,

But your final reward will be heartaches and tears

If you've cheated the guy in the glass.

— Dale Wimbrow (1895–1954)

THE LESSONS OF COVID-19

*"The spiritual path is not a solo endeavor.
In fact, the very notion of a self who is trying to face her/
himself is a delusion. We are in it together and the company
of spiritual friends helps us realize ourselves."*
— *Tara Brach*

As I finish writing this manuscript, we are in the midst of the coronavirus pandemic. It has been a difficult experience for all, and we are learning more about it and all its debilitating effects every day. One thing for certain is that it can have some devastating effects on the mental health of those who are infected by the virus and those who suffer anxiety over the possibility of contracting the disease.

Technology came to the rescue during these difficult times. There are literally thousands of Zoom calls not only in the United States, but all over the world 24 hours a day. These meetings have helped keep recovering people connected. It is interesting that most recovery people I speak to are anxious to get back to meeting in person where there are no distractions, and we make eye to eye contact with each other.

Because of the various lockdowns over the past year and the isolation people are experiencing, there has been an increase in domestic violence and child abuse. There appears to be an increase in anxiety, depression, loneliness, and substance abuse as well.

After months of isolation, these mental health issues are stressing our health systems. What we have learned is that humans do not do well in isolation. We crave connection. The alcoholic, whose thinking is already distorted, has little chance of navigating this time of isolation on his own. All humans benefit from healthy interaction with others. Alcoholics simply cannot do without it if they are to succeed.

I have attempted to point out in this book that alcoholism cannot be treated in a vacuum. Although medication-assisted treatment can be helpful, it is not the only answer to addiction. Alcoholics, like the rest of humanity, need human contact. For the alcoholic it is the answer to long-term sobriety and general mental health. We need others to see us; without them we are doomed.

CONCLUSION

"Sobriety was the greatest gift I ever gave myself."
— *Rob Lowe*

I remain concerned about the move away from inpatient treatment and toward medication-assisted treatment. Insurance companies and pharmaceutical companies are encouraging this move. For insurance it is to reduce costs, and for pharma it is to make money. The pharmaceutical industry sees a vast market and an opportunity to generate enormous profits.

Many years ago, the psychiatric profession moved away from talk therapy and into drug therapy. There have been great advances in treating some mental illnesses with drugs; however, for the most part talk therapy with psychiatrists no longer exists. Pharmaceutical companies have promoted drugs; as a result, doctors no longer see a patient for an hour to talk—now they see a patient for a short time and write a script.

As I've mentioned, the United States has the highest

rate of prescription drug use in the world. According to the 2019 *World Happiness Report*, the US ranks 19—so it seems drugs are not the complete answer; humans need to talk. Many alcoholics start to drink so they can socialize and fit in. It seems like a magic potion—life becomes fun and interaction easy. In the end, most addicts die alone, a slave to their drug or drugs of choice.

Although the addiction doctors who are working in dispensing MAT all tell me that the drugs help the acutely addicted person, none have said they are the answer. Alcoholism is a complex physical, mental, and spiritual malady; putting the alcoholic or addict on a drug barely scratches the surface of treating it. Now more than ever, we need to be able to give patients a path for recovery, and the most important part of that is the human connection we so desperately need. That path was beautifully designed eighty years ago.

My observations are just that; they are not a scientific study. We are cautioned by Bill Wilson not to look for an easier, softer way. This illness is progressive and must be addressed in the myriad ways it affects us and everyone we come into contact with on a daily basis. Without addressing the way we think, which is the root of this illness, we are doomed. My hope is that while medication-assisted treatment might be helpful, those who use it realize that it is far from the answer. If an addict is to survive, then he or she must be brought to self-awareness. Only then can we become fully engaged in life.

The long-term answer to addiction is what Bill Wilson and Bob Smith realized eighty years ago: human connection. We all hunger for it.

ACKNOWLEDGMENTS

I am so grateful to all who have helped me on this path. I have been told that the AA program is a design for living and that it is helpful to all, alcoholic or not, who would like to live a life of peace and serenity.

I am fortunate that my three daughters and my son, who all weathered my alcoholism, are a big part of my life today. My wife would not let us ignore the damage, and gently, over many years, she challenged us to get help and taught us how to communicate with one another. We are a much better family unit now, even though sometimes we still have to step back and look at ourselves. I am grateful to them for their love and devotion. They will never know just how much their support sustains me.

I must thank three of my siblings, Maggie, Peter, and Joe, who had the courage and love to confront me when I was at my worst. It is because of them that I am in recovery today. I am also grateful to my other seven siblings, for they too have been my rudders.

The men and women in my meetings, my sponsors, and

the weekly Caduceus group have all helped me to remain sober. I met Matthew Kelly early in my recovery, and he has been one of the greatest gifts that I have been given. His writings and support have made me a-better-version-of-myself. For all of them I am truly thankful. The path is not straight up. Like every human being, I have had my disappointments and losses, but with these ongoing interactions and my willingness to communicate, my life continues to improve.

Whether you believe in God or not, this is what recovery is about. It is about our spiritual nature and how we can get in touch with ourselves and some force greater than ourselves, and outside of us. We show one another unconditional love without judgment. We share our experience, strength, and hope with those who suffer from addiction so that they might experience the joy of recovery. Bill Wilson and his colleagues promised "reasonable" happiness, and if we can stay connected to our fellow alcoholics and addicts long enough, we eventually realize that is enough. We then understand it is about love of ourselves first, and then love of those around us. We then are available to those who need our help.

What Bill Wilson and Dr. Bob Smith discovered eighty

years ago as the long-term answer to addiction remains the same today as it was then. Although prescription drugs may help early in one's recovery, they are not the solution to the problem. Alcohol and drugs are not the problem—our thinking is, and the only way out is a continuous human connection while we are on this earth.

Finally, when I was at my worst, it was not I who recognized that I was not alright; it was those around me who cared enough to confront me about my behavior. As I was taught, self-knowledge will not save an alcoholic. I needed to reach out and I must continue to do so, if I wish to remain mentally healthy and self-aware. The purpose of this book was to point out that we all need human connection. For the alcoholic it is an absolute necessity. Bill Wilson and his friends gave us that path.

NOTES

1. New York State Office of Addiction Services and Supports, "Standards for OASAS Certified Programs," April 2019, https://oasas.ny.gov/system/files/documents/2019/07/Standards%20for%20OASAS%20Certified%20Programs.pdf.

2. Adriana Rodriguez and Jayne O'Donnell, "New Study Shows How Effective Alcoholics Anonymous Really Is," *USA Today*, March 11, 2020.

3. "Does Alcoholics Anonymous Work?" Vimeo video, 15:09, March 11, 2020, https://vimeo.com/378364390.

4. Rodriguez and O'Donnell, "New Study Shows How Effective Alcoholics Anonymous Really Is."

5. "Does Alcoholics Anonymous Work?"

6. Anahad O`Connor, "Bottoms Up? Maybe You Had Better Not," *New York Times*, July 14, 2020.

7. Emma Seppälä, "Connect to Thrive," *Psychology Today*, August 26, 2012, https://www.psychologytoday.com/us/blog/feeling-it/201208/connect-thrive.

8. Alex Williams, "The New Sobriety," *New York Times*, June 15, 2019.

9. Benedict Carey and Robert Gebeloff, "Many People Taking Antidepressants Discover They Cannot Quit," *New York Times*, April 7, 2018.

10. Howard Markel, *An Anatomy of Addiction: Sigmund Freud, William Halsted, and the Miracle Drug Cocaine* (New York: Pantheon Books, 2011).

11. Nora D. Volkow, "What Does It Mean When We Call Addiction a Brain Disorder?" *Scientific American*, March 23, 2018, https://blogs.scientificamerican. com/observations/what-does-it-mean-when-we-call-addiction-a-brain-disorder/.

12. Volkow, "What Does It Mean When We Call Addiction a Brain Disorder?"

13. Volkow, "What Does It Mean When We Call Addiction a Brain Disorder?"

14. *Alcoholics Anonymous* (New York: Alcoholics Anonymous World Services, 1976), 58.

15. *Alcoholics Anonymous*, Third Edition, page 30.

16. Maia Szalavitz, "Addiction Doesn't Always Last a Lifetime," *New York Times*, August 31, 2018.

ABOUT THE AUTHOR

Dr. J. Anthony Quinn Is a Board-Certified Orthodontist who practiced in Northeastern Pennsylvania for the past 44 years.

For the past 35 years he has been involved with both a recognized 12 step program and a weekly Caduceus meeting that was designed for health care professionals to help them face the special challenges they face when they first become sober.

His experiences with these groups have given him insight into the true nature of recovery. In his book he cautions us be wary of drug assisted treatment as an answer for addiction. The human connection is the answer to successful recovery.

If you wish to write to Dr. J. Anthony Quinn,
your email can be addressed to him at:
observe1020@gmail.com